D0048354

NOTHING TO HIDE

NOTHING TO HIDE

Secrecy, Communication, and Communion
in the Catholic Church

By Russell Shaw

IGNATIUS PRESS   SAN FRANCISCO

Cover art: © iStockPhoto

Cover design by John Herreid

© 2008 by Ignatius Press, San Francisco
All rights reserved
ISBN 978-1-58617-218-3
Library of Congress Control Number 2007928876
Printed in the United States of America ⊗

CONTENTS

INTRODUCTION

*The consequence is clear: we cannot communicate with the
Lord if we do not communicate with one another.*
— Pope Benedict XVI

Let us begin with *The Da Vinci Code*. The book and the
2006 movie were based on the premise that the Catholic
Church engaged in a huge deception about Christ from the
very start. Their commercial success made it clear that many
people either were willing to suspend disbelief long enough
to enjoy the grotesque tale they told or else believed it.

The *New York Times* quoted one moviegoer: "The Catholic Church has hidden a lot of things—proof about the actual
life of Jesus, about who wrote the Bible. All these people—
the famous Luke, Mark and John—how did they know so
much about Jesus' life? If there was a Bible, who created it
and how many times has it been changed?" The newspaper
identified the speaker as a twenty-five-year-old associate director of a Bronx senior center—a Catholic who, it said, "was
baptized and confirmed in the church, went to Sunday school
for six years, and still attends Mass twice a month".[1]

The results of the cover-up of clergy sex abuse are visible
in reactions like this. So are results of many other abuses of

[1] Laurie Goodstein, "It's Not Just a Movie, It's a Revelation (About the
Audience)", *New York Times*, May 21, 2006.

7

secrecy. The *Da Vinci* phenomenon capitalized on mistrust of the Church, and while much of that mistrust is unfair, that does not make it any less real. Even though some people seize on the Church's alleged failures of candor to excuse their own dishonesties, in other cases mistrust is a reaction to real offenses against openness and honesty, past and present. There is an enormous amount of work to do to repair the damage to the Church's credibility. And make no mistake—credibility is crucial to the Church's success or failure in preaching the gospel.

Hence this book.

When I told an eminent theologian I was writing a book about the abuse of secrecy in the Catholic Church and its cousins—lying, stonewalling, happy talk, failure to consult, and the rest—and would appreciate having his advice on sources to consult, he told me to read canon law. "I haven't thought much about secrecy, but it's a canonical question", he explained.

So I read canon law. I found canons dealing with secret records and archives, the seal of the confessional, and the secrecy of the ecclesiastical courts called tribunals that handle marriage cases. All this was interesting, but it was not what I was looking for, and it is not what this book is about.

Nothing to Hide is not concerned with legitimate secrecy of the kind required to protect confidential records and people's reputations. It is concerned with the stifling, deadening misuse of secrecy that does immense injury to communion and community in the Church.

And, despite what my friend the theologian said, that kind of secrecy is a theological problem as well as a practical one. Specifically, it is a problem rooted in ecclesiology, the theology of the Church. The questions it raises boil down to these: What kind of church do we want *our* Church to be, open or closed? What kind of church *should* it be? And how much secrecy is compatible with having such a church?

A kind of inverted logic often enters into the discussion of these questions. The Church is a communion, not a political democracy, it is said; therefore openness and accountability do not count for too much in the Church. But the argument should go just the other way around: the Church is a communion, not a political democracy; therefore openness and accountability are even more important in the Church than they are in a democracy.

In a paper delivered some twenty years ago to a conference for the continuing education of priests, Joseph Cardinal Ratzinger—now Pope Benedict XVI—had this to say about the reality of ecclesial communion:

> Fellowship in the body of Christ and in receiving the Body of Christ means fellowship with one another. This of its very nature includes mutual acceptance, giving and receiving on both sides, and readiness to share one's goods. . . . In this sense, the social question is given quite a central place in the theological heart of the concept of communion.[2]

Among the "goods" to be shared, one might add, it is appropriate and necessary to include, along with materials goods, the goods of truthfulness and honesty.

This is a beautiful vision of the Church. In its own small way, the present book seeks to make a modest contribution to realizing it in the concrete circumstances of the present day, by helping to end the culture of secrecy, first in American Catholicism and then, one hopes, beyond it as well,

---

[2] Joseph Cardinal Ratzinger, "Communion: Eucharist—Fellowship—Mission", in *Pilgrim Fellowship of Faith: The Church as Communion*, ed. Stephan Otto Horn and Vinzenz Pfnur (San Francisco: Ignatius Press, 2005), 69.

and replacing that destructive culture with an open, account-able community of faith.

———#———

Nothing to Hide is organized as follows.

Chapter 1 is an introduction to the nature and dimensions of the problem as it now exists.

Chapter 2 offers a brief historical overview, focusing especially on the First Vatican Council (1869–1870) and the Second Vatican Council (1962–1965).

Chapter 3 examines the abuse of secrecy in the Church's media relations, with particular attention to the ups and downs in the practice of the Catholic bishops' conference of the United States since Vatican Council II.

Chapter 4 discusses issues of internal communication in contemporary Catholicism.

Chapter 5 presents some preliminary reflections relevant to the development of a theology of openness in the Church.

Chapter 6 makes concrete suggestions concerning steps to take in order to foster openness, accountability, and shared responsibility in Catholic life.

The book contains many anecdotes, and there is a reason for that. In speaking about the abuse of secrecy in the Church, I have often encountered denial—the refusal to see, much less admit, that there is much of a problem here. People in positions of authority are particularly likely to react that way. So it is necessary to show in concrete terms that the problem does exist and that it is serious. Anecdotes are a way of doing that. Some of the incidents recorded here are small, even trivial, and some plainly are not. All of them are drawn from real life. Taken together, large or small, they add up to a disturbing picture.

Someone who read a draft of this book complained that I was attributing moral fault to people in leadership positions in the Church. That is a bad misreading of what the book says. The problem examined here—the abuse of secrecy—is a systemic one with a long history. People take it for granted as part of the way we have grown accustomed to doing business. It is not a moral fault, but it is a serious mistake that does the entire Church much harm.

With only a few exceptions, I am speaking in this book about American Catholicism. The Vatican and the Church in other countries have their own histories, their own customs and cultures, and it is not any business of mine to diagnose and prescribe concerning what I understand either imperfectly or not at all. American Catholicism is a different story. I have been an American Catholic all my life, and, based on personal and professional experience, I think I am qualified to speak about the Church's culture of secrecy and the faults and flaws in her structures and practice of communication as I have experienced them.

I encourage others to do the same and in this way make their contribution to the fellowship in the body of Christ of which Pope Benedict speaks.

Several people have offered helpful suggestions in the writing of this book. In a special way I wish to acknowledge the many very useful insights and ideas I received from Dr. Germain Grisez, which have greatly strengthened the book in a number of places and especially in the development of its argument for openness. Needless to say, its weaknesses are my responsibility, not his.

Chapter One

"THE VERY WORST SCANDAL
OF OUR TIMES"

It was the kind of letter every writer likes to get—serious, thoughtful, mellowed by the wisdom of experience.

I had published a magazine article about the growing over-use of secrecy by the bishops of the United States when they gather for their general meetings. In reply, an elderly bishop, nearing retirement at the time, wrote to share his own long experience on this matter and what it had taught him. This, in part, is what he said:

> As a priest formed in the cauldron of the Second Vatican Council, I don't have any reluctance to proclaim truth, even in circumstances that seem difficult. More scandals come from attempting to control access to truth than ever came from honesty and openness.
>
> The very worst scandal of our times in the Church has been the sexual predations of some priests. The attempt to keep such matters secret on grounds of protecting reputations through the years simply allowed the evil to fester and grow. And when the dam of secrecy finally broke—as it always will—the whole Church suffered for its lack of candor.
>
> When [measures to ensure secrecy] are employed because the matter is of such moment that it cannot be entrusted to

13

the *plebs*, that decision seems to contradict not only the conciliar documents on the right to know, [but] it also calls into question the overall role of the lay people to participate in the Church's decisions. (personal communication)

This letter seemed to me then, and seems to me now, an honorable contribution to discussion of a problem seldom recognized and, at least until recently, seldom discussed: the abuse of secrecy in the Catholic Church. I wish more bishops, pastors, religious superiors, administrators of religious institutions, and ordinary Catholics were as open and honest about it as my friend the bishop was. My hope here is to advance this discussion because I care about the Church and want to help her.

Abuse of secrecy is a systemic, structural, and ecclesiological problem, grounded at least in part in an imperfect understanding of the Church herself. It has many sources, including those that operate to produce abuses of secrecy in nonchurch settings, such as government, corporate life, and the military. But because the problem under examination here is secrecy in a *church*, it also arises from and is inseparably linked to a special factor peculiar to churches. Its name is clericalism.

The abuse of secrecy occurs in many areas of Catholic life: finances, the appointment of bishops and pastors, Church governance, and much else. It has a deadening, alienating effect wherever it is present. But the link between clericalism and secrecy can most easily be illustrated in the case of the clergy sex abuse scandal. I have written about clericalism before, and in some circles (mainly clerical ones), I have a reputation of being a bit of a fanatic on the subject. At the risk of reinforcing that impression, let me explain what I mean.

Secrecy and the Clerical Culture

Clericalism in the Church, I once wrote, is "something like the pattern in the wallpaper: it's been there so long you don't see it any more".[1] But visible or not, clericalism and the clericalist culture were at the heart of the sex abuse scandal.

By "clericalism" I mean an elitist mindset, together with structures and patterns of behavior corresponding to it, that takes it for granted that clerics—in the Catholic context, mainly bishops and priests—are intrinsically superior to the other members of the Church and deserve automatic deference. Passivity and dependency are the laity's lot. By no means is clericalism confined to clerics themselves. The clericalist mindset is widely shared by Catholic lay people.

Clericalism did not cause sex abuse, nor did sex abuse cause clericalism. But the connection is very real. Sex abuse in a clericalist social setting naturally takes on a clericalist coloration, making it difficult to keep the two things separate and distinct. To put it simply, the attitudes and behavior patterns tied to clerical elitism time and again came into play when priests were found by their superiors to have engaged in abuse. These attitudes and patterns of behavior made what already was a tragedy for some individuals into a calamity for the entire Church. There is no other way of credibly explaining the actions of bishops known to be decent, intelligent, conscientious men who nevertheless hushed up the shameful crimes of wayward priests and repeatedly transferred some of them to new parish assignments without so much as putting the parishioners on notice.

[1] Russell Shaw, "Clericalism and the Sex Abuse Scandal", *America*, June 3–10, 2002.

As we know now, of course, some bishops were themselves wayward men. Moreover, bishops consistently received astonishingly bad advice from chancery officials, lawyers, psychiatrists and psychologists, and others on whom they relied. And, had others in the Church been let in on the secret, including some who now are vociferous in their criticism of the bishops, they too probably would have agreed that a policy of cover-up, ineffective "therapy", and reassignment made good sense. That reflected the way people thirty or forty years ago generally thought about priests, about the sexual abuse of minors, and about what they saw as the need to protect the Church against the consequences of misbehavior by some clerics.

But, granting all that, the mishandling of bad priests by good bishops unquestionably expressed the prevailing clericalist assumptions of those times. What was a bishop to do with a priest who got into trouble by sexually abusing minors or who by some other form of misconduct had harmed a child? The answer pretty clearly was: protect him to the point of coddling him, let him have time off to rest and pray, send him for therapy, give him a new assignment once the therapists pronounced him an acceptable risk, and, above all, keep the mess quiet by limiting knowledge of what had occurred to the smallest possible circle within the chancery.

Bishops who acted like this were acting reasonably by the standards of the clericalist culture to which they belonged. Wishing to be good servants of the Church, they served the clericalist system. And in the end this system of concealment and illusion betrayed them and the rest of the Church.

In June 2002 the American bishops established an all-lay National Review Board to oversee the implementation of the new, tough policy on sex abuse that the bishops had just adopted. In February 2004 the Review Board published a report on the "causes and context" of the scandal. Titled "A Report on the Crisis in the Catholic Church in the United States", it is indispensable reading for anyone trying to understand this disaster.[2]

One section is devoted to clericalism. It delivers a devastating critique of clericalist culture.

> Some witnesses likened the clerical culture to a feudal or a military culture and said that priests and bishops who "rocked the boat" were less likely to advance. Likewise, we were told, some bishops did not want to be associated with any problem for fear of criticism because problems arose on their watch. As a result, problems were left to fester.

The report left no doubt about the link between clericalism and secrecy.

> In many instances, Church leaders valued confidentiality and a priest's right to privacy above the prevention of further harm to victims and the vindication of their rights. Both confidentiality and privacy are valuable.... But these values should not be allowed to trump the duty to keep children safe from harm.

Clericalism, according to the report, also was to blame for "massive denial" on the part of Church leaders when faced with cases of sex abuse by priests: "Indeed, Church officials seemed to want to keep information from themselves." Finally, contributing to the problem were the "haughty attitude" of some bishops and the practice of placing priests on "a pedestal far above the laity".

---

[2] National Review Board, "A Report on the Crisis in the Catholic Church in the United States", *Origins*, March 11, 2004.

The Review Board also spoke at length about the dual problem of "secrecy and the avoidance of scandal". Faced with cases of abuse, it said, Church leaders "placed too great an emphasis on the avoidance of scandal in order to protect the reputation of the Church". Protecting the faith of the laity probably also helps account for this desire to keep problems "within the family" and out of sight. Church leaders failed to grasp that the problems, unless caught and corrected at the start, would become worse with the passing of time and eventually do even more to undermine people's faith.

There is a telling remark about the priesthood and the laity's view of priests in Edwin O'Connor's novel about an alcoholic priest, *The Edge of Sadness*: "Probably in no other walk of life is a young man so often and so humbly approached by his elders and asked for his advice." [3] In an earlier day—the heyday of clergy sex abuse, it now appears —that was an accurate description of the clericalist mindset and its culture of pretense that led both priests and laity to play at make-believe. Not anymore.

From a certain point of view, clericalism is the clergy's way of surrendering to two temptations that threaten to corrupt every profession and trade. These are the tendency to distort and pervert the solidarity and mutual loyalty that rightly bond its members (doctors covering for incompetent colleagues, honest lawyers closing their eyes to the ethical failings of dishonest ones); and the tendency to hold low expectations and tolerate a lack of accountability in regard to professional responsibility. Secrecy lends support to both.

---

[3] "Which, by the way," the priest-narrator adds, "is almost always received gratefully and forgotten promptly" (Edwin O'Connor, *The Edge of Sadness* [Boston: Little, Brown, 1961], 119).

These temptations also exist in the clerical world. Clericalism reinforces them and makes the clergy more likely to succumb. What is the solution? Bishops and other pastoral leaders—including responsible priests in their relationships with fellow priests—must take the requirements of openness and honesty much more seriously than many have done up to now. Among other things, that means confronting an erring brother and, if confrontation does not work, reporting him to higher authority.

Ethicist Sissela Bok's description of the reaction of people who find out they've been "lied to in an important matter" captures the mood of countless American Catholics confronted with the reality of sex abuse by some priests and the abuse of secrecy by people in authority who systematically covered it up.

> [They] are resentful, disappointed, and suspicious. They feel wronged; they are wary of new overtures. And they look back on their past beliefs and actions in the light of the discovered lies. They see that they were manipulated, that the deceit made them unable to make choices for themselves according to the most adequate information available, unable to act as they would have wanted to act had they known all along.[4]

It would be foolish to imagine these reactions to the sex abuse scandal have magically faded from the American Catholic scene today.[5]

---

[4] Sissela Bok, *Lying: Moral Choice in Public and Private Life* (New York: Random House Vintage Books, 1999), 20.

[5] Nor have Church authorities magically perfected the art of openness. In August 2006, for instance, the Diocese of Springfield, Illinois, released a special panel's report on misconduct, not involving minors, by a former ordinary of the diocese and some other diocesan clergy. It concluded, among other things, that the former bishop had "engaged in improper sexual conduct

In the years since Vatican Council II, the exercise of pastoral authority in the Church has repeatedly been called a form of service. And so it is. But honesty and openness are necessary if the exercise of authority is not to degenerate into paternalistic authoritarianism with a smiling, "pastoral" face. Ending the abuse of secrecy for the sake of clerical manipulation and control is essential to that.[6]

Naming Bishops—Whose Business Is It?

The mishandling of sex abuse by priests in the past is hardly the only example of the abuse of secrecy in the Church. Consider what is known—and what is not—about the process by which men get to be bishops.

There is continuing agitation in some circles today to make the selection process far more open and participatory than it is now. Very likely it should be, but that is not my point at the moment. Here I merely speak of the dearth of information concerning the process as it now works. A Catholic journalist shared this story.

The editor of a Catholic magazine became aware that in many instances lately a new kind of bishop had begun to

---

and used his office to conceal his activities" and had fostered a "culture of secrecy" in the diocese. The report, however, was notable for its opacity and its abstract language, leaving the reader in the dark about exactly what the bishop and others mentioned had done. Perhaps this was necessary to avoid legal complications, but no explanation was offered, and the reader was left to imagine that things were even worse than they were. In such a case, one respects the intention to be open while recognizing that the performance leaves something to be desired. See "Diocese Investigates Clergy Misconduct", *Origins*, August 17, 2006.

[6] For a fuller account of Catholic clericalism, see Russell Shaw, *To Hunt, To Shoot, To Entertain: Clericalism and the Catholic Laity* (San Francisco: Ignatius Press, 1993).

emerge in the United States. These new men tend to be more tough-minded and realistic and more visibly orthodox than a lot of their predecessors had been. Good guys, in other words.

The editor got in touch with me and asked me to do an interview about this with the papal nuncio to the United States—the Vatican ambassador, that is. Everybody knows that the nuncio plays a key role in the selection of bishops, and the editor's thinking was that he might be willing to say whether the criteria now being used accounted for the change she and others had observed.

Now, I have been around awhile, and I did not think anything would come of it. But I told her anyway, "For you, I'll do it." So I gave it a shot.

At that time I went to weekday Mass pretty often at a parish near my home, and priests from the nunciature—the Vatican embassy—frequently came over to say the Mass I attended. I think they wanted to keep their hands in doing pastoral work, and I respect them for that.

One morning after Father X had said the Mass, I went back to the sacristy, introduced myself, and explained what I had in mind—an interview with the nuncio about the selection of bishops. I emphasized that I didn't want him to tell me any secrets, and I certainly wasn't going to ask him to name names. I just wanted a serious conversation with the pope's representative about a subject of great importance to Catholics—the way the leaders of their Church get chosen.

As I was speaking, I could not help noticing that Father X had begun to stare at me as if I were a dangerous lunatic. It made me sort of nervous after a while. When I finished, he said, "I can't help you with that. The nuncio certainly isn't going to oblige you by saying that bishops who are being appointed now are orthodox and bishops who were appointed in the past were not." Believe me, he wasn't smiling when he said that either.

"No, no", I murmured, wanting to reassure him that this wasn't what I was after. But he went on as if he hadn't heard me.

"If you want an interview with the nuncio, you're free to write to him yourself. But if you want my opinion, he'll say no. And if by any chance he *should* talk to you, I guarantee you it won't be the interview you want. He'd speak to you in very positive, very general terms—fluff, in other words—and that is all. Don't quote me on that."

"Then it wouldn't be worth my time or his", I replied. And I wished him good day and left. "It turned out just the way I said it would", I told the editor later. (personal communication)

When Secrecy Is Needed

Secrecy and confidentiality have a necessary, honorable role in human affairs. A world in which no secrets were kept and all confidences were routinely betrayed would be a frightening, dangerous place. People would need to be constantly on guard even in dealing with those nearest and dearest to them.

During the past century, we have had more than a little practical experience of totalitarian states like that. And George Orwell's *1984* remains a compelling parable of life in a place where personal privacy is systematically violated by an omnipresent regime.

> The telescreen received and transmitted simultaneously. Any sound that Winston made, above the level of a very low

whisper, would be picked up by it; moreover, so long as he remained within the field of vision which the metal plaque commanded, he could be seen as well as heard. There was of course no way of knowing whether you were being watched at any given moment. How often, or on what system, the Thought Police plugged in on any individual wire was guesswork. It was even conceivable that they watched everybody all the time.... You had to live—did live, from habit that became instinct—in the assumption that every sound you made was overheard, and, except in darkness, every movement scrutinized.[7]

We have not reached that point, of course, and, God willing, we never shall. But in a time of large-scale identity theft, widespread electronic eavesdropping, unannounced government spying on its citizens, and the awareness that copious information about oneself reposes in data banks of whose very existence one may not be aware, invasions of privacy already have proceeded a great deal further than many people would wish.

Not so long ago, a government bureaucrat, acting without authorization, took home a laptop computer containing personal information, including Social Security numbers, on twenty-six million American military veterans—and the laptop was stolen in a common robbery. Fortunately, it later was recovered; but it is a frightening world in which such an incident can occur.

Not only individuals but institutions and groups can have a need for and a right to privacy. Sissela Bok points out that many joint undertakings require secrecy "for the sharing and working out of certain plans and for cooperative action". Premature exposure would be their undoing. "Many projects

---

[7] George Orwell, *1984* (New York: Harcourt, Brace, 1949), 4.

need both gestation and emergence, both confinement and publicity", Bok says.[8] The challenge is to tell the necessary, helpful secrecy that protects legitimate privacy and confidentiality from the secrecy that is unnecessary and unhelpful—often, even to those who are involved in keeping the secret.[9]

What is true in secular affairs frequently takes on special meaning in the religious sphere. In the early centuries of the Church, for example, the "discipline of the secret" (*disciplina arcani*) was the practice of concealing core doctrines of faith from pagans as a means of self-protection; as a catechetical device, such doctrines were revealed only gradually even to catechumens.

The privilege of being present at the celebration of the Eucharist itself was reserved for those whom baptism had made full-fledged members of the Christian community, while catechumens—non-Christians undergoing instruction—were required to depart before the Mystery was celebrated (a custom revived in recent times as part of the Rite of Christian Initiation of Adults). The purpose of excluding the catechumens was to shield the most sacred realities of Christian belief from observation by persons not yet sufficiently formed to appreciate them and not yet empowered by initiation into the Church's sacramental life to join in celebrating them.

[8] Sissela Bok, *Secrets: On the Ethics of Concealment and Revelation* (New York: Vintage Books, 1983), 23.

[9] Without entering into a discussion of whether the Constitution does or does not implicitly guarantee a right to privacy, it can be said that the privacy of individuals and groups is a crucial principle of life in society. The problem with citing privacy to legitimatize a practice like abortion does not reside in privacy itself but in an individualistic and libertarian understanding of it that gives each person the power to do whatever he likes. Carried to its logical conclusion, this corruption of the idea of privacy renders social life itself impossible.

The lives of martyrs offer paradigmatic examples of how faithful observance of the obligation of secrecy can be a decisive virtue. Martyrs often become martyrs and are honored as such by the Church not only for having courageously proclaimed the gospel and lost their lives as a result, but also for courageously keeping quiet when they might have saved themselves by disclosing information their persecutors wanted.

For instance:

> The two brothers were interrogated under torture, but remained steadfast in refusing to apostatize and in refusing to betray their fellow Catholics....
>
> I honour the Queen, and I will obey her and you in all that is lawful. But on this point you must hold me excused. If I name any person who has harboured me or mention any house where I have found shelter, innocent people will suffer for the kindness they have done me. Such is your law, but for my part I would be acting against charity and justice....
>
> He did take notice that by frailty he had confessed of some houses where he had been, which now he repented him, and desired Mr. Pound to beg pardon of the Catholics therein, saying that in this he rejoiced, that he had discovered no things of secret, nor would he, come rack, come rope.

There are many passages like these in the true stories of these heroes of faith.

When people think about the duty of secrecy in the Church, most likely they think first of all of the "seal of the confessional"—the strict obligation, binding on the priest and on anyone who happens to overhear someone else's confession, to reveal nothing of what is said. Violation of the seal is punished by automatic excommunication, which can be lifted only by the Holy See. The Code of Canon Law says: "The sacramental seal is inviolable; therefore it is a crime for a confessor in any way to betray a penitent by word or in any other manner or for any reason" (canon 983). And again: "A confessor is absolutely forbidden to use knowledge acquired from confession when it might harm the penitent", while a person in authority can "in no way use for external governance knowledge about sins which he has received in confession at any time" (canon 984).

There are obvious human reasons for this great emphasis on the secrecy of the confessional. The trust the sinner shows in confessing to the priest deserves respect. Violating that trust would discourage him and others who knew what happened from confessing again to that priest or perhaps any other. The social solidarity of the Church as a community of faith and love would be seriously compromised. But there also is a deeper reason. In this sacrament the priest acts as a stand-in—a kind of proxy—for Jesus Christ himself. In the inner reality of the sacrament, Catholics believe, it is not merely the priest but Jesus who hears the confession; the priest would be doing something gravely wrong in revealing what was intended primarily for the ears of Christ.

These considerations also apply in various degrees to other confidential exchanges in a religious context, such as spiritual direction and pastoral counseling. Here the obligation is much like the obligation regarding the confidentiality of attorney-client and physician-patient conversations.

A special case, similar to these, is the "manifestation of confidence" practiced by some religious who, following the rule of their institute, periodically open their souls to their religious superiors. It is dismaying to learn that, at the time of this writing, the confidentiality of this privileged form of spiritual disclosure had been challenged in a civil court in Alaska.[10] It also is dismaying that, as of early 2006, the New Hampshire state legislature had before it a bill to remove the priest-penitent privilege in cases of suspected child abuse.[11] Similar legislation was introduced there by the same legislator and defeated in 2003. The Catholic League for Religious and Civil Rights termed the proposal "an unconstitutional encroachment by the state on religion".

Conclaves for the election of popes are conducted in strict secrecy, with stern penalties provided for those who violate it. (Violations and leaks do occur, of course, and cardinals apparently are responsible for them. Perhaps that reflects the vaunting sense of entitlement felt by some officeholders at the top levels of the clerical culture.) Pope John Paul II put in place particularly stringent security procedures for the conclave, including measures to prevent electronic bugging. Some people marvel at this emphasis on secrecy, but if they were more familiar with the history of papal elections they might not. Secular authorities often intervened in papal elections of the past to influence the result. The current rules, procedures, and penalties are meant to shield the cardinal-electors from a recurrence of pressure and coercion.[12]

[10] "Abuse Case Puts Jesuit Confidentiality on Trial", *National Catholic Reporter*, January 6, 2006.

[11] "New Hampshire Bill Targets Confessional", Catholic League for Religious and Civil Rights, news release, January 30, 2006.

[12] Pope John Paul's apostolic constitution *Dominici Gregis* requires cardinals participating in the conclave to subscribe to an oath that reads in part: "In a particular way, we promise and swear to observe with the greatest fidelity and with all persons, clerical or lay, secrecy regarding everything that in any way relates to the election of the Roman Pontiff and regarding what occurs in the place of the election, directly or indirectly related to the results of the voting ... and never to lend support or favor to any interference, opposition or any other form of intervention, whereby secular authorities of

Over and above these specifically religious settings where secrecy is a sacred duty and a right, the Church has good reasons for practicing secrecy and confidentiality in a variety of other circumstances involving respect for the good name of persons, a decent sense of discretion and privacy, and the legitimate desire not to be placed at a competitive disadvantage in business or legal dealings.

Where the Church is obliged to practice secrecy, says a Vatican document on communications, "the rules normal in civil affairs equally apply." [13] The *Catechism of the Catholic Church* similarly recognizes the legitimacy and binding character of professional secrets, except "in exceptional cases where keeping the secret is bound to cause very grave harm to the one who confided it, to the one who received it or to a third party, and where the very grave harm can be avoided only by divulging the truth". Even if it has not been confided "under the seal of secrecy", the *Catechism* adds, "private information prejudicial to another is not to be divulged without a grave and proportionate reason." [14]

The claims of confidentiality often deserve respect in legal battles over sex abuse claims. Priests against whom charges have been made but not proven, abuse victims who prefer not to be publicly identified as such, and bishops struggling to balance a variety of legitimate but conflicting interests, including protecting diocesan assets against doubtful claims

---

whatever order or degree or any group of people or individuals might wish to intervene." The last time intervention is known to have occurred was during the conclave of 1903, when the emperor Franz Joseph attempted to blackball one of the cardinals.

[13] Pontifical Commission for Social Communications, Pastoral Instruction on the Means of Social Communication, *Communio et Progressio* (May 23, 1971), no. 121.

[14] *Catechism of the Catholic Church*, no. 2491.

and legal fishing expeditions, can all have compelling reasons to resist demands for the disclosure of confidential information.

In the final analysis, apparent conflicts over whether to disclose information can be settled only by the exercise of prudence, pastoral sensitivity, and the fortitude needed to do what is right—disclose or not disclose, as the case may be—even in the face of criticism. The abuse with which this book is concerned is *unnecessary, self-serving* secrecy, not the discretion and confidentiality that are sometimes morally obligatory.

The Trouble with Secrecy

The Catholic bishops of the United States in June 2002 committed themselves to "transparency and openness" regarding sexual abuse of minors by priests, deacons, and other Church personnel.[15] They have not done that in regard to other areas of the Church's life. In fact, as we shall see below, the United States Conference of Catholic Bishops for some years has been moving in the other direction in its manner of conducting business, while the practices of individual dioceses appear to vary greatly.[16]

---

[15] Article 7 of the Charter for the Protection of Children and Young People adopted by the bishops on June 14, 2002, at their meeting in Dallas, Texas, states: "Each diocese/eparchy will develop a communications policy that reflects a commitment to transparency and openness. Within the confines of respect for the privacy and the reputation of the individuals involved, dioceses/eparchies will deal as openly as possible with members of the community" (*Origins*, June 27, 2002). The charter is silent on the subject of sexual misbehavior by *bishops*.

[16] In April 2006 the financially hard-pressed Archdiocese of Boston released a financial report described as the most detailed ever published by any diocese. Although this is commendable, it took a huge sex abuse scandal and a

Unnecessary secrecy in the conduct of Church affairs does great harm in many ways. Here are four.

1. *Secrecy conflicts with openness and honesty and, practically speaking, makes accountability all but impossible.*

The lack of openness by Church leadership is a particularly serious problem in the context of American Catholicism. Americans take it for granted that, just as much as possible, public business affecting everyone should be carried on publicly, precisely so that the performance of those in charge can be evaluated, and criticized and corrected as necessary, and so that other members of the community have the information they need to do their part in working for the community's common good. Even when secrecy is necessary on grounds of national security, it is regarded as a regrettable exception to the general rule. Backroom dealing of all kinds is viewed with suspicion.

Curiously enough, however, even in this day and age these principles are not clearly established and accepted in the Church. The duty of the pastors to be open and honest with the faithful is not universally acknowledged and certainly not universally observed. This is a continuing source of dismay and resentment among Catholics accustomed to openness and honesty in other areas of their lives. We shall return to this subject below.

---

financial crisis in Boston to bring about this result, and in the absence of similar pressures other dioceses have not done the same. One archbishop, commenting on what Boston had done, remarked that people would find it hard to interpret some of the information in a comprehensive report. This points to a need to explain such information, not withhold it.

2. *Secrecy easily becomes an instrument of manipulation and control.*

Calling the manipulation of persons "a threat to human freedom and dignity", the moralist Bernard Häring, C.SS.R.,
writes:

> As long as the social and religious *elites* [emphasis in orig-
> inal] think in a paternalistic way and consider the general
> public only as objects or as inferior people to be taught and
> informed, they betray their proper role.... Genuine lead-
> ership in the process of liberation and humanization means
> dialogue, co-responsibility and education in a common pro-
> cess of growth towards maturity and discernment.[17]

We are still very far from realizing this ideal. The fact that
much manipulation is rationalized as being in the best interests of those manipulated does not make it any more
acceptable.

3. *Secrecy contributes to ignorance about the Church on the part
of her members.*

In a discussion not long ago with some other Catholics, including several bishops, I argued that steps should be taken to
create new structures of shared responsibility in and through
which lay Catholics could participate with bishops, clerics,
and religious in formulating the Church's position on matters of social and economic justice. (The idea flourished for
a time in the years after the Second Vatican Council, but it
largely died out for reasons to be examined later.)

In response to my plea for the laity, a Church official—a
layman himself and a highly sophisticated and dedicated

---

[17] Bernard Häring, *Ethics of Manipulation: Issues in Medicine, Behavior Control and Genetics* (New York: Seabury Press, 1975), 24.

person—said with a laugh, "They're too dumb." He meant
it as a joke, but he was making a serious point, undoubtedly based on his own repeated experience: when given
the opportunity to participate, Catholic lay people very often
turn out not to know enough about the history, institutions, and processes of the Church to make a useful contribution to policy setting.

I had to agree with that, and I mumbled something about
the evident need for "catechesis" to correct the problem.
What I did not say was that using the laity's knowledge
deficit as an excuse for excluding them from an adult role
in Church affairs has the character of a self-fulfilling prophecy. The less the laity are told, the more ignorant they
become; the more ignorant they become, the less qualified
they are to participate. At some point this vicious circle
must be broken.

4. *Secrecy contributes to alienation, anger, rebellion, and a rejection of authority that go far beyond reasonable criticism.*

A lay theologian teaching at a Catholic university in the
United States claims that the oppression of the American
Catholic laity bears a "striking" resemblance to racism and
sexism. Employing the categories of liberation theology, he
writes: "If the vocation of the laity is to human freedom,
their existential predicament in today's church is that they
are in chains." [18]

There is something deeply offensive about likening the
grievances of middle-class American Catholics to the suffering of the world's marginalized and oppressed. Rhetorical

[18] Paul Lakeland, *The Liberation of the Laity: In Search of an Accountable Church*
(New York: Continuum, 2002), 186.

overkill like this is symptomatic of a situation in which persistent abuses—including the abuse of secrecy—have sent some critics over the edge. Here is at least part of the human reality underlying declining church attendance, a startling drop-off in the rate of Catholics marrying in the Church, and the widespread rejection of Church teaching by many lay people.

What the Polls Say

Public opinion polls for many years have produced voluminous data illustrating the interlocking problems in American Catholicism. The latest in a series of surveys sponsored by the liberal *National Catholic Reporter* stretching (up to this time) over eighteen years from 1987 to 2005 found that 34 percent of Catholics attend Mass weekly or more often, 30 percent attend between one and three times a month, and about a third go to Mass less than once a month. Twenty-seven percent of the married Catholics said their marriages were not approved by the Church. Other research indicates that 57 percent do not go to confession as often as once a year.

Purdue University sociologist James D. Davidson reported "sizable generational differences" on a number of matters.

> Sixty-three percent of pre–Vatican II Catholics [born before 1940] strongly agreed that the sacraments are essential to their relationship with God. About half of the Vatican II generation [born between 1941 and 1960] and the post–Vatican II generation [born between 1961 and 1978] strongly agreed, and only 38 percent of Millennial Catholics [born between 1979 and 1987] strongly agreed....
>
> Generation also affects Mass attendance rates. While 60 percent of pre–Vatican II Catholics attend Mass at least once a week, only about one-third of Vatican II Catholics and

one-quarter of post–Vatican II Catholics do. Only 15 percent of Millennials go to Mass on a weekly basis.[19]

As they had done before, the researchers asked a series of
questions concerning whether one could be a "good Catholic" without accepting various elements of the faith. The
yes answers—one *can* be a good Catholic without believing
in (or in some cases, doing) these things—included 23 percent who saw no problem with denying Jesus' physical Res-
urrection; 36 percent who felt the same about the Real
Presence of Christ in the Eucharistic species at Mass; 44
percent in regard to giving time and money to help the
poor; 58 percent when it came to "obeying the church
hierarchy's teaching regarding abortion", the same figure for
giving time or money to the parish; 66 percent on "obeying" the teaching on divorce and remarriage; 67 percent
on having their marriages approved by the Church; and 75
percent on "obeying" the teaching on birth control. Fully
76 percent agreed that good Catholics do not need to go
to weekly Mass.

Those are the numbers. Here is a straw in the wind. A
Catholic layman who shares my interest in the situation of
the laity in the Church and who has spent more than a
quarter century in administration at a community college
in the Midwest wrote me to say the young adults he knows
"are not interested in what we are talking about. Religion
is not a concern of theirs." For good measure he added
that even those who sometimes engage in worship "don't
want to commit to a parish group".

It would be silly to blame all this on the abuse of secrecy
in the Church. Many factors combine to produce the present

[19] James D. Davidson, "Belief in Church as Mediator Slips", *National Catholic Reporter*, September 30, 2005.

troubling picture. But it also would be foolish to close one's eyes to an obvious fact: the current unhealthy condition of American Catholicism mirrors a body of people with diminished knowledge of and commitment to what the Church asks of them in matters of belief and practice. This has at least something to do with the ignorance and alienation associated with the systematic abuse of secrecy. To put it bluntly, the Catholic Church in the United States is not communicating effectively with a very substantial portion of her nominal members. That is having the destructive results one might expect. More openness is not the total solution, but it is part of it.

Failures in Communication

The abuse of secrecy is part of a larger failure of communication that takes several forms.

Sometimes it is happy talk by the authorities. Problems are "swept under the rug" or else dismissed as insignificant; the bright side of things receives exaggerated emphasis; everything will turn out for the best, we are told; silver linings abound. During the turmoil of the years immediately after the Second Vatican Council—from the late 1960s through the 1970s and beyond—people in responsible positions in the Church repeatedly shrugged off defections from the priesthood and religious life, noisy theological and practical dissent, and the mounting evidence of institutional decline as no more than the growing pains of renewal.

Another part of the problem of internal communication is the unwritten rule that lay people should not correct the clergy (at least, not to their faces; Catholics are notorious for their gossip, sometimes harmless and sometimes not, about priests). To some extent, the rule may be breaking down today, here and there at least; yet even now lay people who voice criticism to their clergy do so at their own risk. Here is an example.

A woman visiting a strange parish attended a Mass at which the priest committed several more-or-less serious liturgical abuses. After Mass she approached him and, smiling, shook hands politely. She tells what happened next.

> "Father, you certainly say an enthusiastic Mass," I said. "But you're not allowed to omit the creed."
>
> He began to be agitated and said, "What's your name?" I introduced myself and said we were visiting. "I'll pray for you, Father," I said, still smiling. He said he would pray for me too. Then I added as mildly as I could, "Father, you teach your people to be disobedient when you disobey the Church."
>
> At that point something bizarre happened.
>
> He began grimacing, opening his mouth very wide and then closing it like someone on a plane trying to clear his ears. He did it several times, twisting his head and neck at the same time. Then he leaned over and said in my ear, "You know what, honey? You're full of it." He walked away, raising his hand over his shoulder. I had turned away, but my husband said it looked like he gave me the single-digit salute.[20]

No one enjoys being criticized. The priest in this incident found the woman a pain in the neck, and maybe she was. But she also was right in what she said, and she was entitled, perhaps even obliged, to say it. Pastors, stated Vatican II, "should recognize and promote the dignity and responsibility of the laity in the Church. They should willingly

[20] This account by Mary Ann Kreitzer appeared in the Fall 2005 issue of *Les Femmes: The Women of Truth*, a newsletter published in Woodstock, Virginia.

use their prudent advice."[21] Apparently we have a way to go on that.

I write as a conservative Catholic who is committed to the welfare of his Church and convinced that the abuse of secrecy is bad for it. Many of my fellow conservatives appear not to share my concern: orthodoxy and morality matter more to them. And, as a matter of fact, they also matter more to me. But the historical record strongly suggests that where secrecy is systematically abused, orthodoxy and morality sooner or later will suffer.

That is a central lesson of the scandal of sexual abuse of children and young people by priests. Openness and candor would not have prevented the scandal, but they would have made it a lot less traumatic than it turned out to be. We need to give openness and honesty a try lest something else equally as bad, or even worse, should occur in the future. And also because, I am convinced, an honest, open church is the kind of church God wants the Catholic Church to be.

---

[21] Vatican Council II, Dogmatic Constitution on the Church, *Lumen Gentium* (November 21, 1964), no. 37.

Chapter Two

"MONSTROUS DOCTRINES AND PRODIGIOUS ERRORS"

A brief study like this cannot provide a full-scale history of secrecy in the Catholic Church. But a few highlights from modern times—the nineteenth and twentieth centuries—do help sketch the recent background of the problem that now exists. An incident from the career of John Henry Newman is a good place to start.

Scholarly and deeply spiritual though he was, Newman had a surprising knack for touching off heated controversies that focused on himself. Perhaps it was his habit of speaking his mind. In early 1859, as the recently appointed editor of a Catholic journal called the *Rambler*, he exhibited this unusual talent yet again.

Shortly before he arrived on the scene, the *Rambler* in January and February of 1859 had published two articles arguing that British Catholics ought to cooperate with a royal commission looking into the condition of elementary education. Unfortunately for the *Rambler*, the British bishops had taken the opposite view at their meeting the previous November, though up to that time they had neglected to say so publicly.[1] Be that as it may, the result was a change of editors that brought Newman on board.

[1] In a letter of March 8, 1859, Bishop Ullathorne of Birmingham declared it to be "absolutely unnecessary that the reasons for our own actions should

The May issue of the *Rambler*, the first under his direction, carried the now publicly known judgment of the British bishops on the royal commission question, together with an unsigned editorial comment stating in part: "We do unfeignedly believe ... that their Lordships really desire to know the opinion of the laity on subjects in which the laity are especially concerned. If even in the preparation of a dogmatic definition the faithful are consulted, as lately in the instance of the Immaculate Conception, it is at least as natural to anticipate such an act of kind feeling and sympathy in great practical questions." [2]

Mild as these sentiments may seem now, they were highly inflammatory for some people at the time. The upshot was a May 22 meeting between Newman and his bishop, William Bernard Ullathorne, at which there occurred a famous exchange later recalled by Newman: "He said something like 'Who are the laity?' I answered ... that the Church would look foolish without them." Newman and the bishop agreed it would be best for everyone if the eminent convert resigned after the magazine's next issue, scheduled for July.

That July issue carried a long essay—almost a short book—entitled "On Consulting the Faithful in Matters of Doctrine". It is not the intention here to summarize its argument or recount the furor it produced in British Catholic clerical circles, with consequences highly prejudicial to Newman's reputation and career. Suffice it to say that the author's thesis,

be explained & that the Catholic community should be informed of the grounds of our proceedings" (quoted in John Coulson's introduction to John Henry Newman's *On Consulting the Faithful in Matters of Doctrine* [New York: Sheed and Ward, 1961], 16). Nevertheless, the bishops did eventually announce their position on the royal commission, and Bishop Ullathorne published a pastoral letter explaining and defending it.

[2] Quoted by Coulson in ibid., 8.

based on an analysis of the Catholic response to the Arian heresy in the fourth century, was that what lay Catholics believe about truths of faith is a relevant datum shedding light on the belief of the Church. That view was controversial at the time, though now it is commonly taken for granted.

At the close of "On Consulting the Faithful", Newman provided a long excerpt from an account written by one of his Oratory colleagues, Father J. D. Dalgairns, of the public response to the announcement that the Council of Ephesus in A.D. 431 had declared the Virgin Mary to be rightly called *Theotokos*, Mother of God, thus making a point of great importance to both Christological and Mariological doctrine. "Men, women, and children, the noble and the low-born, the stately matron and the modest maiden, all crowd round the Bishops with acclamations", Dalgairns wrote. "They will not leave them; they accompany them to their homes with a long procession of lighted torches. . . . There was but little sleep in Ephesus that night; for very joy they remained awake; the whole town was one blaze of light."

To this picturesque description Newman appended the following comment of his own:

My own drift is somewhat different from that which has dictated this glowing description; but the substance of the argument of each of us is one and the same. I think certainly that the *Ecclesia docens* is more happy when she has such enthusiastic partisans about her as are here represented, than when she cuts off the faithful from the study of her divine contemplations, and requires from them a *fides implicita* in her word, which in the educated classes will terminate in indifference, and in the poorer in superstition.[3]

---

[3] Newman, *On Consulting the Faithful*, 106.

Making allowances for the many differences of time, place, and circumstance, that is a substantial part of the case against secrecy—and in favor of open and honest communication—in the Church today. Newman desired to see the laity consulted, about doctrine and much else. But if the laity are to provide useful feedback, they need to be kept informed. And even more: secrecy is bad, and openness is good, because secrecy cuts off people from ecclesial communion while openness invites them in.

Anti-Catholicism, the Press, and the Church

In this matter as in so much else, Newman was ahead of his time. The nineteenth century was an era of top-down ecclesiastical authority and entrenched clericalism. An era, too, when the Church and the papacy felt themselves—and they often truly were—besieged by enemies, including the new phenomenon of a widely circulated popular press that was often rabidly anti-Catholic and antipapal in its views. There was little chance that Church leaders would take a friendly view of freedom of the press in these circumstances.

Pope Gregory XVI emphatically did not. In the 1832 encyclical *Mirari Vos*, after deploring the rise of "indifferentism" in religion and morality, Pope Gregory wrote:

> Here we must include that harmful and never sufficiently denounced freedom to publish any writings whatever and disseminate them to the people, which some dare to demand and promote with so great a clamor. We are horrified to see what monstrous doctrines and prodigious errors are disseminated far and wide in countless books, pamphlets, and other writings which, though small in weight, are very great

in malice. We are in tears at the abuse which proceeds from them over the face of the earth.[4]

Similarly, Pope Pius IX in the 1864 encyclical *Quanta Cura*, which accompanied the famous Syllabus of Errors, echoed Pope Gregory on the dangers of freedom of expression and freedom of the press. "In these times," he declared, "the haters of truth and justice and most bitter enemies of our religion, deceiving the people and maliciously lying, disseminate . . . impious doctrines by means of pestilential books, pamphlets and newspapers dispersed over the whole world."[5] It seems not unreasonable to suppose that the Syllabus of Errors had freedom of the press in mind—along with many other errors—when it concluded by anathematizing the proposition that "the Roman Pontiff can and should reconcile and adapt himself to progress, liberalism, and the modern civilization."[6]

Jacques Maritain contends that in taking this line, Pope Gregory and Pope Pius meant to reject the absolutizing of freedom of expression as an end in itself,[7] and it is helpful to bear this suggested explanation in mind. Certainly one must bear in mind the very real attacks on the Church that were then taking place. But even when considered in the most favorable light, such views seem eccentric today—not least, in light of Pope John XXIII's inclusion among the human rights listed in the encyclical *Pacem in Terris* of "a right to freedom in investigating the truth,

---

[4] Pope Gregory XVI, *Mirari Vos* (On Liberalism and Religious Indifferentism) (August 15, 1832), no. 15.

[5] Pope Pius IX, *Quanta Cura* (Condemning Current Errors) (December 8, 1864), nos. 3, 7.

[6] Pope Pius IX, Syllabus of Errors (December 8, 1864), no. 80.

[7] Jacques Maritain, *Integral Humanism: Temporal and Spiritual Problems of a New Christendom* (New York: Charles Scribner's Sons, 1968), 182.

and—within the limits of the moral order and the common good—to freedom of speech and publication ... the right, also, to be accurately informed about public events".[8]

It deserves repeating that the papal negativism of the nineteenth century reflected a time when anticlerical newspapers were prominent in the assault on the Church and the papacy then under way throughout Europe. "Through much of the century," writes American journalist Richard Ostling, "the press, especially in Italy and France, had distorted and often ridiculed the Catholic church."[9] A not dissimilar situation also existed in the United States, where waves of anti-Catholic nativism greeted the growing numbers of Catholic immigrants from Ireland, Germany, and other European countries.

When a mob inflamed by lurid tales of nameless horrors in the nunnery burned a convent of the Ursuline sisters in a Boston suburb in 1834, it marked the start of violence or the threat of violence aimed at immigrants and Catholics—who, very often, were the same people—in many places. The Irish quarter of Boston was burned in 1837, and there were reports of church burnings throughout the country in the 1840s. Archbishop John ("Dagger John") Hughes, the pugnacious archbishop of New York, in 1841 warned that the city would be "a second Moscow"—New York would go up in flames—if nativists attacked Catholic churches there. Time and again, the press helped to foment animosities that led to such events.

[8] Pope John XXIII, *Pacem in Terris* (Peace on Earth) (April 11, 1963), no. 12.

[9] Richard N. Ostling, *Secrecy in the Church: A Reporter's Case for the Christian's Right to Know* (New York: Harper and Row, 1974), 81.

The Battle over Lay Trusteeism

The experience of lay trusteeism did much to move Church leadership in the United States in the direction of a closed, clericalist approach to governing the Church. Dating back to an era when Catholicism itself was illegal, the trustee system represented a response in almost all states to legal requirements concerning ownership of church property that themselves reflected widely held suspicion of hierarchically organized churches.

Among Catholics the system also reflected the influence of the example supplied by Protestant congregationalism and American republicanism, as well as the incitement of renegade priests and the intransigence of the trustees themselves. Charles Morris says the lay trustees of Catholic churches "particularly in the earliest days, acted pretty much like Protestants"—they managed the money and the property and "as often as not, hired and fired pastors".[10]

Not surprisingly, serious conflict between lay trustees and Church authorities erupted in a number of places, including New York, Philadelphia, Charleston, and Norfolk. The trustee system was eventually stamped out by a dual process of changing state laws and enacting stringent canonical regulations, which the bishops adopted in a series of Church councils during the century. But the struggle left behind it heightened clericalism, mistrust of the laity, and a belief in closed, clericalist governance. We shall see more about these matters later.

The effect these developments and others had on at least some of the laity is suggested by the angry words of a

[10] Charles R. Morris, *American Catholic: The Saints and Sinners Who Built America's Most Powerful Church* (New York: Times Books, 1997), 74.

particularly strong-minded layman: the convert, author, and social critic Orestes Brownson. He discerned a deadening anti-intellectualism at work.

> In our historical reading we have found no epoch in which the directors of the Catholic world seem to have had so great a dread of intellect as our own.... There is a widespread fear that he who thinks will think heretically. The study, therefore, of our times is to keep men orthodox by cultivating their pious affections with as little exercise of intelligence as possible.... The true policy, in our judgment, would be not to yield up thought and intelligence to Satan, but to redouble our efforts to bring them back to the side of the church, so as to restore her to her rightful spiritual and intellectual supremacy.[11]

Wise words from an angry man.

The First Vatican Council (1869–1870)

Many currents in nineteenth-century Catholicism converged in 1869–1870 at the First Vatican Council. Some were for the good, including the strong support now apparent in the worldwide Church for the primacy of the pope's teaching and governing authority. Other currents, however, were not so positive: for example, the preference for secrecy in Church affairs that came naturally to clerical leaders of the day; the confusion, conflict, and resentment to which secrecy so often gave rise; and the ingenious

[11] Orestes Brownson, "Catholic Polemics" (1861), in *The Brownson Reader*, ed. Alvan S. Ryan (New York: P.J. Kenedy and Sons, 1955), 334–35.

countermeasures that interested parties found for circumventing concealment and failure to communicate.[12]

In many ways, Vatican I was a brave act of defiance on the part of Pius IX. Encircled by the forces of the Italian nationalist movement now casting covetous eyes on the Eternal City itself, Pio Nono sought to send the message that, no matter what befell the papacy's temporal power, its spiritual power would be undiminished and even enhanced.

Strict secrecy enveloped Vatican I from the start. So determined was the pope about this that the director of the Vatican Secret Archives, who for years had been working on an edition of the documents of the Council of Trent, was forbidden to show it to any bishop, lest the openness of the sixteenth-century council put the secrecy of the nineteenth-century council in an unfavorable light.[13] Even clergy "proctors", whom absent bishops designated to represent them in Rome, were excluded not just from the Council but from discussions of their respective national hierarchies.[14]

The secrecy policy was quixotic: for the first time in the history of the Church, a general council now was being watched by an international press corps made up of

[12] This account of media aspects of Vatican Council I is drawn largely from Owen Chadwick, *A History of the Popes, 1830–1914* (Oxford: Oxford University Press, 1998).

[13] Ostling, *Secrecy in the Church*, 82.

[14] The American bishops found a way around this by authorizing proctors who also were appointed as theological advisors to bishops to attend their sessions. Of the two proctors from the United States, one, Father Isaac Hecker, C.S.P., founder of the Paulists, took advantage of this concession, while the other, Father John Ireland, the future archbishop of Saint Paul, Minnesota, did not. See Marvin R. O'Connell, *John Ireland and the American Catholic Church* (St. Paul, Minn.: Minnesota Historical Society Press, 1988), 124.

"journalists hungry for copy",[15] their curiosity further piqued by the subject matter of the deliberations, papal infallibility. But the Vatican failed to grasp the implications. Owen Chadwick writes:

> The government of the Papal States, which lived in a world of several decades before the time, had no idea of this new circumstance of society. They accepted the ancient doctrine that as all proceedings were confidential no one ought to be told anything. Cardinal Antonelli [the secretary of state] kept sedulously away from anyone who wrote casual articles for the press.
>
> The Curia did not realize the elementary truth that an assembly of 600 to 700 people could not hide what it did if it was in any way controversial. Bishops talked to their friends, or to their ambassadors. Several bishops felt that the imposed clause of silence, which they had not voted on themselves, did not bind them.[16]

The results were predictable: "The solemn secrecy of the Council became a sieve." Documents were leaked. Rumors circulated. Insider accounts proliferated, and these naturally tended to emphasize whatever was controversial. Eager for a story and angry at being kept at arm's length, the journalists drank it all in and regurgitated it in reportage "with a hostile slant" until they lost interest in the proceedings.

Into this vacuum of reliable information stepped two remarkable figures: the Englishman Sir John Acton and the Frenchman Louis Veuillot. What happened next illustrates the truth of Sissela Bok's remark that the leaking of information "has a symbiotic relationship with secrecy.... Without secrecy there would be no need to leak information.

[15] Chadwick, *History of the Popes*, 205.
[16] Ibid., 206.

As ... secrecy grows and comes to involve more people, the opportunities to leak from within expand; and with increased leaking, [those in charge] intensify their efforts to shore up secrecy." [17] Yet even as they do, Bok points out, the people in charge not uncommonly turn to selective leaking of their own. Thanks to the secrecy policy at the Vatican Council, the Church and the world were now to receive an early but surprisingly sophisticated lesson—two lessons, in fact—in leak-generated spin.

It began with Acton. John Emerich Dalberg Acton in 1870 was a well-born, cosmopolitan, thirty-six-year-old liberal Catholic with credentials as a historian and sometime journalist. He opposed the power of the Curia, the centralizing of authority in the papacy, the pope's preoccupation with retaining the Papal States, and the proposal to define the dogma of papal infallibility. Significantly, in Munich he had been a student and friend of Father Johannes Döllinger, a Church historian who was a prominent figure in European liberal Catholic circles. [18]

Acton came to Rome determined to block the infallibility definition if he could. Exploiting his excellent contacts among the local political and social elites as well as among French, German, and English bishops who belonged to the anti-infallibility minority within the Council, he dispatched a series of letters to Döllinger in Munich, which the historian edited and published in the *Allgemeine Zeitung* under the title "Letters from Rome on the Council by Quirinus". The "Letters from Rome", Chadwick says, "portrayed

[17] Sissela Bok, *Lying: Moral Choice in Public and Private Life* (New York: Random House Vintage Books, 1999), 217.

[18] After Vatican I, Döllinger refused to accept the doctrine of papal infallibility and led opposition to it; he was excommunicated by the archbishop of Munich in 1871 and died in 1890 unreconciled with the Church.

the Council from the viewpoint of the most hostile among
the Minority and gave Europe a picture of an unscrupulous
Majority tyrannizing over minds and consciences." [19] The
official secrecy helped make Acton's dispatches a key source
of contemporary public knowledge about Vatican I and also
"controlled the picture of it for years to come, even among
historians".

Louis François Veuillot set up shop in Rome with the
intention of doing something similar for the conservative
side. Fifty-seven years old at the time, the Frenchman had
since 1843 edited the newspaper *L'Univers*, a journal of un-
compromisingly pro-papal views that strongly supported
papal infallibility and the temporal power of the pope. Because
its editorial position on the latter question conflicted with
French government policy, Veuillot was arrested in 1844
and forced to suspend publication from 1860 to 1867.

Recognizing that he had a loyal supporter in Veuillot,
Pius IX directed a monsignor to keep this friendly journalist primed with inside information about what was going
on at the Council. The resulting reports denounced the
minority and steadfastly upheld the majority position. But
they had results very different from those produced by Acton.
Whereas the Englishman "affected the view of interested
Europe", Veuillot "touched French and Italian clergymen
and a faithful band of French laymen and laywomen; he
caused French priests to question their bishop if he was a
member of the minority." [20]

On balance, it would be hard to say which side played
this particular game more successfully, the pope and Veuillot

[19] Chadwick, *History of Popes*, 206.

[20] Ibid., 207. The author attributes the anecdote about the leaks to Veuillot to a biography of the Frenchman by Eugene Veuillot.

or Acton and Döllinger. Each side achieved at least some of
what it wanted. How well the Church as a whole was served
is another matter. Richard Ostling sums it up:

> The secrecy policy ... did not work. Information on the
> council was rife, but it was necessarily a mix of truth and
> rumor. None of the clergy and laity of the church could be
> at all sure what was going on and why. The atmosphere of
> distrust could not be dispelled. . . . Historians of the council
> agree that the secrecy tactic was utterly disastrous.[21]

Secrecy tactics often are. Secrecy and its violation at the
First Vatican Council set a disturbing pattern in the conduct of Church affairs that would persist for many years.

Decades of Transition

Yet adaptations and innovations dictated by changing circumstances had, in their own way, also begun. By turning
to Louis Veuillot and *L'Univers* to tell his side of the story
during Vatican Council I, Pope Pius IX signaled a nascent
awareness that communication via mass media had its uses.
Two decades earlier, in fact, the Jesuit-edited weekly *Civiltá
Cattolica* had been established with papal approval as a semi-
official voice of the Holy See, while the daily *L'Osservatore
Romano* was launched in 1861 by a group including the
Papal States' deputy minister of the interior Marcantonio
Pacelli, grandfather of the future Pope Pius XII. In time it
became the official Vatican newspaper. On the whole,
Church leadership still did not like or trust the press and
continued to regard press freedom as an insidious error of
modern times; but the leaders also had grasped that the

[21] Ostling, *Secrecy in the Church*, 83.

press was here to stay and had begun to employ it after their own fashion.

Owen Chadwick calls Pope Leo XIII (1878–1903) the first occupant of the Chair of Peter to understand "that the press, even when it was Catholic, was a fourth estate, and to begin to treat it accordingly".[22] True, Leo XIII continued to insist that it was "quite unlawful" to demand, defend, or grant unconditional freedom of speech or publication, "as if these were so many rights given by nature to man"; but he permitted the toleration of these liberties, and he acknowledged that it is "not of itself wrong to prefer a democratic form of government"[23]—of which, he no doubt knew as well as anyone, free speech and a free press are essential elements.

Gradually, the new thinking took hold. In the middle years of the twentieth century, Pope Pius XII, grandson of the co-founder of *L'Osservatore Romano*, spoke often about the new media of communication and praised the service of the press to society. He also endorsed the principle of public opinion in the Church, saying: "Something would be lacking in her life if she had no public opinion. Both pastors of souls and lay people would be to blame for this."[24] Pope John XXIII continued in this line and carried it further. As we saw above, the encyclical *Pacem in Terris* (1963) recognized "freedom of speech and publication" as human rights; these rights in turn were linked to duties, Pope John pointed out, so that, for example, "the right to be free to seek out the truth" was seen to involve

---

[22] Chadwick, *History of the Popes*, 329.

[23] Pope Leo XIII, encyclical *Libertas Praestantissimum* (On Human Liberty) (June 20, 1888), nos. 42, 44.

[24] Pope Pius XII, address to editors of Catholic periodicals, February 17, 1950.

"the duty to devote oneself to an ever deeper and wider search for it".[25]

As a result, Richard Ostling says, by the time of the Second Vatican Council the outlines of a theology of social communication could be discerned in this series of papal statements. Among its elements were these:

> Information is essential in modern society, because it enables the citizen to understand situations and to make responsible decisions. Access to information is justified, because it improves individuals and the community, but to do this information must be ethical, sensitive to the nature of man, true, factual, and objective. Sin and untruth can be caused by omission as well as by commission.... Information should not be degraded into propaganda, appeal to man's passions, or arouse one group against another. Information must stop short of harming a person's right to good reputation and to legitimate secrecy in his private life. Not all information is good for all people—youth in particular should be protected—so the common good must be respected.[26]

Note that these sound principles concerned information *in civil society*; except for Pius XII's words about public opinion, little had as yet been said about information and openness *in the Church*. Still, it was now only a matter of time before people would realize that, other things being equal, sound principles of life in civil society might also apply in the Church; it was only a matter of time, too, before these particular principles would begin to be applied there.

[25] Pope John XXIII, *Pacem in Terris*, nos. 12, 29.
[26] Ostling, *Secrecy in the Church*, 116.

The Second Vatican Council (1962–1965)

The attempt to impose secrecy at Vatican Council I reflected the situation of a Church besieged. The communication policy and practice at Vatican Council II mirrored the conflicted state of mind of a Church that now desired engagement with the modern world yet continued to be burdened with attitudes from the past.

The Council's approach to these matters was mixed and, at the start, more or less disastrous. Vatican II predictably was more of a media event than any previous ecumenical council in history—both because of its own importance and for the simple reason that, with the only partial exception of Vatican I, "media" in the contemporary sense hadn't existed at the time of previous councils.

Nine hundred journalists had been accredited by the Council's press office when the first session got under way in the fall of 1962. By the time the session ended, the number had risen to 1,255. Not all were professional journalists; some were clerics residing in Rome who managed to persuade Catholic newspapers to designate them as their correspondents so that they could enjoy the prestige of being journalists. But even making allowance for this semiprofessional group, the press corps was very large, and the interest it manifested in the doings of the great assembly was of "unprecedented intensity".[27]

Well before the ecumenical council began, Pope John XXIII expressed guarded but friendly interest in the needs of the journalists who would cover it. In June 1961 he told

[27] Hilari Raguer, "An Initial Profile of the Assembly", in *The Formation of the Council's Identity: First Period and Intersession, October 1962–September 1963*, vol. 2 of *History of Vatican II*, ed. Giuseppe Alberigo and Joseph A. Komonchak (Maryknoll, N.Y.: Orbis Books, 1997), 222.

curial officials involved in preparatory work that he did not want to "forget the journalists". It was important for the press to understand the real nature of the Council, which was "neither an academy of science nor a parliament" but an assembly of the world's Catholic hierarchy convoked to discuss "the ordinary life of the Church and the good of souls". "Special respect and reserve" were required on the part of journalists, but it was understandable that the Council should interest the press.[28]

In October 1961, Pope John received journalists in audience. Taking the occasion to promise that everything possible would be done to provide them with information about the Council, he said:

> In fact, we are fully conscious of the precious service that the press will be able to perform in making the Council known in its true light, and in making it understood and appreciated by the public at large as it deserves to be. Indeed, it would be most unfortunate if, for lack of sufficient information, or for lack of discretion and objectivity, a religious event of this importance should be presented so inexactly as to distort its character and the very goals which it has set for itself.[29]

A month later, however, Pope John told the Central Preparatory Commission: "There are some deliberations which necessarily ... must remain veiled in silence." [30]

Apparently those in charge of arrangements for the Council took the pope's words about veiling in silence more to

---

[28] Quoted in Rev. Ralph M. Wiltgen, S.V.D., *The Rhine Flows into the Tiber: A History of Vatican II* (Devon, England: Augustine Publishing, 1979), 30.
[29] Ibid.
[30] Ibid.

heart than what he had said about helping journalists get
the story straight.

Vatican II opened on October 11, 1962. A few days before,
Cardinal Amleto Cicognani, the secretary of state, had blessed
and formally inaugurated the expanded Council Press Office.
Located near Saint Peter's and equipped with modern facilities, the office was to issue 176 news bulletins and 141
backgrounders before the Council ended more than three
years later. Documents were produced in Italian, French,
English, German, Spanish, Portuguese, Polish, Arabic, and
Chinese. The director of the press office, Monsignor Fausto
Vaillanc, reported at the outset to Archbishop Pericle Felici,
the Council's secretary general.

One view of events in the early days of Vatican II holds
that the Roman Curia, seeking to prevent the formation of
public opinion on topics under discussion, imposed a black-
out on meaningful news about what the assembly was
doing.[31] This is possible, but in the absence of evidence
there's no knowing whether it is true. What transpired can
just as well be explained by the we've-always-done-it-this-
way mentality of people accustomed to doing business in a
certain manner—an attitude reinforced in this case by the
unexamined assumptions of clericalist culture. In any case,
the result, as one writer points out, was to spotlight "a glar-
ing contradiction: on the one hand, the very strict obligation to preserve secrecy that was imposed on the fathers of
the Council (article 26 of the Regulations for the Council),
and, on the other, the establishment of a press office, the
obvious purpose of which was to serve as a source of news".[32]

[31] See Raguer, "Initial Profile", 28.

[32] Jan Grootaers, "Ebb and Flow between Two Seasons", in Alberigo and
Komonchak, *History of Vatican II*, 2:552.

Curialists were not the only ones who were suspicious of the media. "Most of the Council Fathers who came to Rome distrusted the press", says priest-journalist Ralph Wiltgen. "They believed they would be misquoted, and therefore refused to meet and cooperate with journalists they did not know." [33]

Whatever the reason or reasons may have been, the performance of the Council Press Office was highly unsatisfactory to journalists at the start. Consider the situation: bishops sequestered in Saint Peter's under strict secrecy rules; a large international press corps clustered a few hundred yards away and increasingly frustrated at not getting the story it had come for. Father Wiltgen credits Monsignor Vaillanc with making "heroic" efforts to provide information,[34] but to no avail: press office bulletins were famously uninformative. Their worst feature was that they gave no names; thus the bulletin covering the first interventions on the liturgical schema read: "Of the fathers who asked to speak, twenty intervened this morning, some to defend the schema, others to attack it." [35] After some loosening up occurred in response to complaints, the press office itself is said to have been in danger of being closed for violating secrecy.

As had happened at Vatican Council I, the first big breakthrough came as a result of leaks—this time, to the French Catholic daily *La Croix*. Starting with the seventh general congregation, the newspaper became so specific in reporting on who had spoken and what had been said that it was taken for granted *La Croix* either had a correspondent on

[33] Wiltgen, *Rhine Flows*, 34.

[34] Ibid., 31.

[35] Bulletin of the fourth general congregation, October 22, 1962. Quoted in Raguer, "Initial Profile", 225.

the inside or was getting tips from a French *peritus* acting at the direction of the French hierarchy.

Declaring that this development meant "secrecy had utterly disappeared"—something for which secrecy's defenders roundly condemned *La Croix*—a Spanish journalist suggests that the episode should be viewed in a more complex light.

> If I myself had to pass judgment on the facts and their results, I would completely absolve *La Croix* of this "sin," which was so immensely useful to bishops and journalists during the months in Rome and of decisive usefulness to all who are today writing the history of the first session of the Council. I would give a different answer if I were asked about the disadvantage which this dispensing of information to only one journalist caused to other French and to foreign reporters, simply because they committed the offense of writing in neutral journals or in the Catholic journals of hierarchies which took a different attitude toward secrecy. Every monopoly is unjust, and so is a monopoly on news when the exclusivity does not result from the skill or efforts of the reporter but from a privileged situation in which he is placed by circumstances or prejudice. And that is how *La Croix* became a small island in the invigorating world of companionship and mutual help that was established among the majority of journalists at the Council.[36]

Another part of that invigorating world was composed of the thirteen centers of information and documentation set up and maintained by national hierarchies and religious institutes. Among these, Wiltgen says, the "most elaborate, most influential and most regular" was sponsored by the bishops of the United States. It "might well be regarded as one of

[36] Quoted in ibid., 230.

that hierarchy's greatest contributions to the Council", he adds.

> The panel during the first session regularly numbered eleven members, all experts on subjects related to the Council's work—dogmatic theology, moral theology, sacred Scripture, ecumenism, council history, canon law, liturgy, seminaries, etc. These experts would clarify definitions and positions, and provide the press with background material on matters under discussion in the Council hall on any one day. As the Council progressed, these briefings were increasingly well attended.[37]

Father Wiltgen, who was director of the information service of the Divine Word Fathers, also describes the method he hit upon for getting reluctant bishops to speak meaningfully in public about the Council without violating the secrecy rule.

> The solution reached was actually very simple. Instead of asking a Council Father to speak about what was going on in the Council hall, I would merely ask him to state in practical terms the needs and wishes of his own diocese in regard to the matter currently under discussion. This did not violate secrecy, and was still topical information for the press. For it was clear that what a bishop might say in this connection would echo views that he, or someone else, was voicing in the Council hall.[38]

No account of the breakdown of secrecy at Vatican II would be complete without mention of the insider accounts by Xavier Rynne—the American Redemptorist priest Francis X. Murphy, C.SS.R.—which caused a sensation in ecclesiastical circles in the United States when they appeared in

[37] Wiltgen, *Rhine Flows*, 33.
[38] Ibid., 34.

the *New Yorker*. Articles and books by Rynne and others giving a detailed picture of Vatican II, albeit one frequently tilted in favor of the Council liberals, soon began telling the Council's story to the world.

During the months between the first and second sessions of Vatican II, official and unofficial meetings were held to devise ways of relaxing the secrecy rule and bringing the Council's information procedures in line with reasonable professional standards. Describing this as a time of "decisive progress", one writer attributes it to the authorities' growing recognition that "the very existence of a Church gathering that intended to be pastoral depended in large measure on the transmission of its message to the public".[39]

What the Council Said

So much for policies and procedures bearing on secrecy and openness. What did the Second Vatican Council say and teach about these things? The answer is: directly—not much; indirectly—a great deal.

The first place one naturally turns is Vatican II's Decree on the Means of Social Communication, *Inter Mirifica*, adopted December 4, 1963. Although the decree has historical significance in that it marks the first time the Church at this level had spoken about the phenomenon of modern mass communication, *Inter Mirifica* nevertheless is commonly dismissed as the weakest of the Council's sixteen documents. It was widely unpopular, to such an extent that three Catholic journalists—Robert Kaiser of *Time*, John Cogley of the *New York Times*, and Michael Novak of the *National Catholic Reporter*—

[39] Grootaers, "Ebb and Flow", 552.

lobbied against it and circulated a joint statement of opposition accompanied by a testimonial from four Council
theologians declaring their critique "worthy of consideration". Also circulated was a document signed by twenty-
five Council fathers who urged rejection of the decree.[40]
In the event, *Inter Mirifica* passed: 1,598 for and 503 against;
this was the largest negative vote received by any of the
Council documents.

Looking back on these events today, it is hard to see what
all the fuss was about. The Decree on the Means of Social
Communication obviously has nothing blindingly original
to say, but neither is it the disaster it was made out to be.
On the whole, it is likely to strike the contemporary reader
as a workmanlike treatment that takes a constructive view
of the media and offers generally sound advice. Its greatest
weakness is a failing common to Church documents not
only then but now: it is free in saying what the secular
world and its institutions should do but sparing in criticism
of the Church.

For example, a passage addressed to "civil authorities"
declares that "the progress of modern society" requires "a
true and just freedom of information".[41] Very good, one
thinks—until it becomes clear that the document is silent
about freedom of information in the Church. As we shall
see, this subject was not to be treated for another seven and
a half years, until finally it was taken up in 1971 in a pastoral instruction from the Pontifical Commission (later,
Council) for Social Communications.

---

[40] The theologians were Father John Courtney Murray, S.J.; Father Jean
Danielou, S.J.; Father Jorge Mejia; and Father Bernard Häring, C.SS.R. See
Wiltgen, *Rhine Flows*, 133–36, for an account of these events.

[41] Vatican Council II, Decree on the Means of Social Communication,
Inter Mirifica (December 4, 1963), no. 12.

More important for the development of the Church's thinking in this area were two of the major documents of the Second Vatican Council: the Pastoral Constitution on the Church in the Modern World, *Gaudium et Spes*, and the Dogmatic Constitution on the Church, *Lumen Gentium*.

The importance of *Gaudium et Spes* in this context lies in its central theme of engagement with the world. No Church which declares that "the joy and hope, the grief and anguish of the men of our time, especially those who are poor or afflicted in any way, are the joy, the hope, the grief and anguish of the followers of Christ"[42] can remain insensitive to the requirement that communication among human persons be open and honest.

As for the Constitution on the Church, its ecclesiology of communion assumes the existence of relationships among the members of the Church that can be realized only through the practice of openness and accountability and that definitively rule out clerical elitism and the abuse of secrecy. The structure of the Church is hierarchical by divine constitution, but also

> [t]here is, therefore, one chosen People of God: "one Lord, one faith, one baptism" (Eph. 4:5); there is a common dignity of members deriving from their rebirth in Christ.... Although by Christ's will some are established as teachers, dispensers of the mysteries and pastors for the others, there remains, nevertheless, a true equality between all with regard to the dignity and to the activity which is common to all the faithful in the building up of the Body of Christ.[43]

[42] Vatican Council II, Pastoral Constitution on the Church in the Modern World, *Gaudium et Spes* (December 7, 1965), no. 1.

[43] Vatican Council II, Dogmatic Constitution on the Church, *Lumen Gentium* (November 21, 1964), no. 32.

Among all the products of the immediate conciliar milieu, however, Pope Paul VI's encyclical on the Church *Ecclesiam Suam*, published August 6, 1964, may be the most important for the issue of secrecy and openness in the Church. Section 3 of the encyclical, titled "The Dialogue", is particularly relevant. Here Pope Paul speaks about God's dialogue with the human race, about the Church's dialogue with the world and with people of other faiths and other Christian denominations, and finally about dialogue in the Church.[44]

The Pope is careful to insist on the "hierarchic constitution" of the Church and on the respective obligations of authority and obedience arising from it. But he also expresses an "ardent desire" that dialogue among Catholics be "full of faith, of charity, of good works", as well as "intimate and familiar", with the character of "a dialogue between members of a body, whose constitutive principle is charity".

> By obedience, therefore, in the context of dialogue, we mean the exercise of authority in the full awareness of its being a service and ministry of truth and charity, and we mean the observance of canonical regulations and respect for the government of legitimate superiors in the spirit of untroubled readiness as becomes free and loving children. . . .
>
> It is, therefore, our ardent desire that the dialogue within the Church should take on new fervor, new themes and speakers, so that the holiness and vitality of the Mystical Body of Christ on earth may be increased.
>
> Anything that makes known the teachings of which the Church is both custodian and dispenser receives our approbation. We have already mentioned the liturgy, the interior

[44] See Pope Paul VI, encyclical *Ecclesiam Suam* (Paths of the Church) (August 6, 1964), nos. 113–17.

life and preaching. We could also add: schools, the press, the social apostolate, the missions, the exercise of charity.... And we bless and encourage all those who, under the guidance of competent authority, take part in the life-giving dialogue of the Church, priests especially and religious, and our well-loved laity.[45]

If the Vatican II years produced a charter for openness, honesty, and the avoidance of unnecessary secrecy in Catholic life, it was this.

[45] Ibid., nos. 115–16.

Chapter Three

MEDIA MATTERS

As the American bishops streamed through the lobby of a Capitol Hill hotel one weekday morning in November 1999 heading for escalators to the subterranean ballroom where their semiannual general meeting would take place, the agenda item foremost on their minds—as well as the minds of journalists mingling with them—was a document described as an "application to the United States" of an apostolic constitution Pope John Paul II had issued nine years earlier.

Titled *Ex Corde Ecclesiae*, "From the Heart of the Church", that papal statement dealt with the touchy subject of the Catholic identity of Catholic colleges and universities. Most Catholic college and university presidents and liberal Catholics in the United States did not like it. They considered it an infringement on the freedom from accountability to the Church's Magisterium that they had come to take for granted as a prerogative of Catholic higher education in the last thirty years and now regarded as part of the natural order of things.

The bishops had been fretting over *Ex Corde Ecclesiae* ever since the pope had inconveniently published it. At one point they had adopted another "application" document, but the Vatican turned it down. Too weak, the Holy See said; try again.

So now they were trying again with the draft of a substantially stronger document. As things turned out, the results of the voting were not even close. The leadership of the bishops' conference had tested the sentiment of the house in a secret, closed-door session the day before and, finding it acceptable, allowed a debate and vote in open session to proceed. The bishops thereupon adopted the new, tougher document by a whopping 223 for, 31 against. Finally American Catholics had some clear standards from the hierarchy for measuring how well Catholic colleges and universities were living up to their duty to be Catholic.

A few days after this meeting ended, somebody with a good reason for wanting to know e-mailed me to ask if I had the names of the thirty-one bishops who had voted no. I had covered bishops' meetings for years, and before that, I had been in charge of media relations for the episcopal conference, yet the question took me by surprise.

After all, the bishops' conference does not disclose that kind of information. When votes are taken in public (as distinguished from votes that may occur in executive sessions), the results are released; but unless particular bishops care to say how they voted, that piece of information remains unknown. (Realistically, of course, if a bishop argues strongly for or against something during open debate before a vote, it is easy to guess how he voted in the end. But guessing is obviously different from knowing for a fact because his vote is a matter of record. In any event, most bishops *do not* speak during any given debate, so there's no telling where these silent members of the hierarchy stand.)

"I really don't know", I e-mailed back to the person who had raised the question. "Sometimes you have a pretty good idea, but unless individuals tell you how they voted, you can't be entirely sure. People at the bishops' conference won't say, and I don't think even they know."

The questioner let it go at that, but the incident got me thinking: Is this really a desirable state of affairs? When the American Catholic bishops, gathered in a public general assembly of their national organization, make a decision of great importance to the entire Church, *shouldn't* people be told how individual bishops voted? Aren't there good, even compelling, reasons for doing that?

We shall return to this question a little later and see that it has no easy yes or no answer. That makes it eminently worth discussing.

Secrecy Does Not Work Anymore

The voting procedures of the national conference of bishops are the tip of the iceberg of official secrecy in the Church. Some years ago Archbishop Diarmuid Martin (then on the staff of the Vatican's Council for Justice and Peace, and now archbishop of Dublin, where he gets generally good marks for trying to move troubled Irish Catholicism from the doldrums of sex abuse and clericalism into a more positive relationship with the world) stated an important principle: "Negotiating things behind the scenes just doesn't work anymore." As it happened, he was talking about the World Trade Organization, not the Church. But the principle fits both: secrecy does not work so well anymore. People want to be let in on the *process* as well as the *result* of decisions that affect their lives.

To some extent, at least, it was this realization that moved the U.S. bishops in 1971 to open most parts of their semi-annual general meetings to direct coverage by the media,

68 *Nothing to Hide*

along with direct observation by official observers. (More on this below.)

The decision placed the Americans in the forefront of bishops' conferences of the world in regard to openness. To this day, bishops' conferences in other countries typically meet behind closed doors and announce what they have decided (if they announce it at all) only sometime after the fact. To get a feeling for what that means, imagine Congress voting behind closed doors on measures whose contents—in fact, whose very existence—came to light only in the carefully censored pages of the *Congressional Record*.

But the American bishops still do some mighty strange things. Consider the *Ex Corde Ecclesiae* debate and vote in November 1999. As noted, the leadership of the bishops' conference, fearful of having a public vote if there was any serious chance of a document so strongly desired by the pope going down in flames, first staged an unannounced, off-the-record, secret discussion in closed session. Only when it was clear that the *Ex Corde Ecclesiae* document would pass handily did the leadership go ahead with a public debate and vote.

It can be argued that this was a responsible way of proceeding. Catholics would have been upset—would they not?—to see their bishops saying no to a document the pope wanted. Very likely many would. But along with being upset, this group also would have been angry at the bishops. So whom were those closed doors shielding the crucial secret debate from prying eyes and ears really meant to protect—the pope, the Catholic people, or the bishops? Moreover, regardless of whether the manner of proceeding was or wasn't responsible, what are we to make of the fact that there was no public explanation—no acknowledgment even—of what was going on? Would it be fair to call this an episcopal shell game?

What about those thirty-one bishops who voted against the document intended to bring the norms of a papal document into play in Catholic higher education in the United States? Following up on the inquiry I had received, I asked the bishops' conference in Washington whether anyone even knew their names. The answer was no. When there is a written vote at a bishops' meeting, an official explained to me, the bishops mark their ballots but do not sign them; then they put the ballots in envelopes, which they do sign, so that there will be a record of who voted—but not how—in case absent bishops must be polled to get the two-thirds majority of the entire membership canonically required on some matters. Before the votes are counted, the anonymous ballots are separated from the signed envelopes. "The ballots are retained at the conference," the official told me, "but since they are unsigned, there's no record of how each individual bishop voted." More recently, the bishops have adopted electronic voting at their general meetings, with the results of each ballot flashed almost immediately on a giant screen. The anonymity is even more absolute in this way.

The reasons for the anonymity of these voting procedures is no mystery. Like the secrecy at a conclave of cardinals held to elect a new pope, not telling how particular individuals vote protects them against second-guessing and retaliation when they get back home. This may make it easier for them to vote their consciences. But by shielding them against public observation, the practice also shields them from the need to account for what they have done. A bishop can vote as he likes—he can even skip votes if he wishes—serene in the knowledge that no one will be able to blame him for the result. There will be no career-threatening criticism from Rome and no nagging by those annoying Catholics, both conservative and liberal, who write bishops impertinent letters raking them over the coals.

Insulation like this is convenient for a bishop, but its advantages for the Church are questionable. To anticipate an objection: no, the Catholic Church is *not* a democracy, and bishops are *not* elected representatives of the People of God. But in this day and age, who would care to argue that the accountability of pastors to people (in a sense to be discussed in chapter 5) is not an important principle in the life of the Church? What form could such an argument possibly take?

But, someone also might object, how voting is handled at a bishops' meeting is not a good example of the abuse of secrecy. As was acknowledged above, there is something to be said both for and against secrecy in this particular case. That is just the point. There *is* something to be said on both sides. Usually, though, only the claims of secrecy get a hearing in the inner sanctums where decisions are made. There often *is* a case for secrecy in the conduct of Church affairs; but before opting for secrecy, it would be good if the authorities weighed the claims of openness. Usually they do not. Concealment is taken for granted.

Bishops are hardly the only culprits in this matter. The abuse of secrecy is common at the Vatican, in religious orders and Church-related institutions of all kinds, and in parishes. But the ups and downs of policy and practice by the bishops' conference of the United States provide material for an illuminating case history concerning the rocky relationship of the Church and the media over many years.

Communicating with the media and communicating with the people of the Church are not the same thing, but in practice they're inseparable. American Catholics learn what their bishops are doing at the national level via the news media. Or else they do not learn at all. And while not learning sometimes is their own fault, sometimes it is because the bishops arrange things that way.

Let us turn, then, to the tangled tale of how the bishops' meeting was opened. And how, after many years of reasonably successful openness, it began to be closed again.

Opening the Bishops' Meeting

When I came to the U.S. bishops' conference in late 1969 to head what then was called the National Catholic Office for Information (the organization's media relations office, in other words), the relationship between the bishops and the media appeared headed for an all-time low. The Second Vatican Council had generated enormous journalistic interest in the Church and her leaders. Developments since Vatican II, including the publication in the summer of 1968 of Pope Paul VI's controversial, prophetic encyclical condemning contraception, *Humanae Vitae*, and the explosion of orchestrated dissent, greatly increased this interest. The American bishops as a group seemed to have little or no idea of how to handle the media situation that now faced them.

A lot of the tension between the hierarchy and the press focused on the bishops' general meetings. These had been held annually in November for many years, behind the closed doors of an auditorium in Caldwell Hall on the campus of the Catholic University of America. (A spring meeting, rotating from city to city, was added after 1966.)

Before Vatican II, journalists mostly ignored the bishops' meetings. The only reporter present was a self-effacing, gentlemanly individual from the bishops' own Catholic news service. Hour after hour he sat patiently outside that auditorium's closed doors, waiting in case one of the bishops were to pop out and hand him something they wanted released.

That had changed dramatically by November of 1969. The bishops had left their campus meeting site, moved to a downtown Washington hotel (for many years, the Capital Hilton, a few blocks up Sixteenth Street from the White House), and begun inviting reporters to cover their meeting. Many did. The results were disastrous.

The meeting was closed. A bishop—and, later, two priests—briefed journalists periodically about what was happening, but the reporters regarded these official briefings with suspicion.[1] The meeting of the previous November, at which the bishops deliberated over their collective response to *Humanae Vitae*, featured demonstrations by some alienated priests and strenuous efforts by some members of the press—more or less successful, I was told—to eavesdrop on the bishops by electronically bugging their meeting room. Adding to the woe, shortly before I came on board, the principal briefing officer, an auxiliary bishop from Minnesota whom the reporters liked, quit the priesthood and declared himself a birth control dissenter; he married not long after that.

Acting on the advice of counsel from the world of commercial public relations, the bishops experimented at the spring meeting in 1969 with a system that involved staged

---

[1] Even so, Richard Ostling says, the briefings allowed reporters to "get enough leads to piece together what was happening" in the meeting. When reasonably accurate accounts of the closed-door sessions began to appear in some newspapers, that upset some traditionalists "who remembered the days when the bishops spoke with an artificially united voice through prepared statements, and could come to their conferences without public notice" (Richard N. Ostling, *Secrecy in the Church: A Reporter's Case for the Christian's Right to Know* [New York: Harper and Row, 1974], 35).

presentations for journalists about Church-sponsored programs for which the bishops hoped to get favorable publicity. These dog-and-pony shows were supposed to keep
the press usefully occupied and out of mischief while the
real meeting took place in secret. The reporters weren't
amused. The experiment was soon scrapped.

Walking into this snake pit in the fall of 1969 with little
understanding of what had been happening in the last few
years, I was appalled at what I found. The reporters who
covered the bishops were hostile and suspicious. The bishops were defensive, angry, and remote. It was a situation
crying out for change.

Soon after the November meeting, I sent a long mem-
orandum to the general secretary of the bishops' conference, Bishop Joseph Bernardin (later famous as archbishop
of Chicago and chairman of the bishops' committee that
produced a much-discussed pastoral letter on nuclear deter-
rence, war, and peace). In the memo, I critiqued the meeting from a communication perspective and tried to explain
what was wrong.

The big problem was the secrecy. When I described the
setup to a psychiatrist, he remarked that by inviting reporters to cover their meeting and then locking them out of it,
the bishops were being provocative. This was a surefire way
to infuriate the press. Whether I used the term "provocative" in my memo to Bishop Bernardin I do not recall, but
I certainly tried to convey the idea: the closed-door policy
was hurting the bishops; they were angering the press for
no good reason; and the journalists were paying them back
with hateful coverage. For their own sakes, the bishops ought
to throw open those closed doors.

Bishop Bernardin offered no promises, but he didn't tell
me to drop the idea. I had the clear impression I was free

to work for change if I cared to do that. Fortunately, some of my colleagues at the bishops' conference felt as I did— and, it soon developed, so did an encouraging number of bishops. The project to open the bishops' meeting had begun.

Over the next two years the bishops' relations with the media didn't improve. The general meeting remained the major friction point. On one occasion a reporter from a daily newspaper hid in the meeting room to listen in on the bishops; another time, he came in dressed as a waiter. Pinpricks like this helped keep the issue alive for everyone.

The result was a series of proposals from bishops' committees and a series of votes by the body. The first time around, a recommendation to open parts of the meeting to journalists fell two votes short of the two-thirds majority that was needed. The second time, the vote was 51 yes's and 148 no's. But the idea did not die. An ad hoc committee chaired by an Indiana bishop named Raymond Gallagher came to the general meeting in November 1971 with a proposal to open the meetings to designated observers *and* the press. On separate votes, the observers got the bishops' blessing (169–76), while the reporters were allowed in less enthusiastically (144–106).

The new system went into effect in April 1972 in Atlanta.

Cardinal John Krol of Philadelphia, a conservative voice in the hierarchy, was president of the bishops' conference by then. Two days before the meeting, the bishops' administrative committee assembled as usual to review the meeting agenda. Cardinal Krol presided. At the coffee break, he summoned me to a corner of the room, waved a sheet of paper at me, and said, "I just got this message from Rome. They're very worried at the idea that the bishops are going to allow reporters in. They want me to prevent it. You know very well that I opposed the idea from the start. But the bishops voted for it, and it's my job as president of the conference to see that their decision is carried out—*and I will*."

The cardinal, a large, imposing man, paused and fixed me with a glare that I took to be only partly humorous. "I bet you think that's funny", he said.

Richard Ostling, who covered that 1972 meeting for *Time*, describes what happened two days later.

> Sometimes history is made in almost humdrum fashion. There was no particular tingle of excitement at 9:30 A.M. on April 11, 1972, as 75 of us reporters filed past uniformed guards into a large meeting room of Atlanta's Sheraton-Biltmore. The meeting we were covering turned out to be relentlessly routine. Despite that, the event was extraordinary. The bishops of the Catholic Church in the United States were opening their deliberations to the church and secular press, and to 23 invited observers from the clergy, religious orders, and laity. This had never before been permitted in the U.S., or hardly anywhere else, in modern times. The U.S. bishops' move to an open-door policy was the end of an era in which secrecy was virtually an unquestioned fact in policy formulation.[2]

Still, Cardinal Krol managed to get his own back, after his own fashion. At the start of the meeting, after the bishops had prayed and taken care of preliminaries, the cardinal rose to speak. He spoke rapidly and at length—in Latin! Nervous coughing and the shuffling of papers could be heard from the press section. After a while he stopped and turned to the side of the room where the reporters sat. He wore a wicked grin.

[2] Ostling, *Secrecy in the Church*, 30.

"We told you we'd let you in", he said. "We didn't tell you what language we'd talk."

What Caused the Change?

Even at the time, it was hard to say why the bishops changed their minds. Perhaps they were tired of being pestered by reporters, staff, and some of their own. Perhaps it had begun to sink in that they were hurting themselves. But something else may also have played a part: the publication in early 1971 of the Pastoral Instruction on the Means of Social Communication. *Communio et Progressio* was its Latin name, meaning "Unity and Advancement".

This important document was the work of a Vatican office called the Pontifical Commission for Social Communications that had been established following Vatican Council II. It was mandated by the Council's own Decree on the Means of Social Communication, *Inter Mirifica*.[3] To help write it, the pontifical commission called on some of the Church's top communication specialists from around the world. The result was a strong, comprehensive, forward-looking treatment of communications and the Church that was approved in its entirety by Pope Paul VI and was confirmed with his authority.

Passages relevant to secrecy in the Church are found in part 3, which bears the title "The Commitment of Catholics in the Media". Affirming that "communication and dialogue among Catholics are indispensable"[4] and recalling the much-quoted statement by Pope Pius XII that

[3] See Vatican Council II, Decree on the Means of Social Communication, *Inter Mirifica* (December 4, 1963), no. 32.

[4] Ibid., no. 114.

"something would be lacking in [the Church's] life if she had no public opinion",[5] the document says that those who exercise authority in the Church should "take care to ensure that there is responsible exchange of freely held and expressed opinion among the People of God". The authorities should "set up norms and conditions for this to take place", it added.[6]

From the fact that public opinion in the Church is "essential", the document draws a necessary conclusion: "Individual Catholics have the right to all information they need to play their active role in the life of the Church."[7] Three crucial paragraphs elaborate on this principle.

The normal flow of life and the smooth functioning of government within the Church require a steady two-way flow of information between the ecclesiastical authorities at all levels and the faithful as individuals and as organized groups. This applies to the whole world. To make this possible various institutions are required. These might include news agencies, official spokesmen, meeting facilities, pastoral councils—all properly financed.

On those occasions when the affairs of the Church require secrecy, the rules normal in civil affairs equally apply.

On the other hand, the spiritual riches which are an essential attribute of the Church demand that the news she gives out of her intentions as well as of her works be distinguished by integrity, truth, and openness. When the ecclesiastical authorities are unwilling to give information or are unable to do so, then rumor is unloosed, and rumor is not a bearer of the truth but carries dangerous half-truths. Secrecy should therefore be restricted to matters that involve the

[5] Ibid., no. 115.
[6] Ibid., no. 116.
[7] Ibid., no. 119.

good name of individuals, or that touch upon the rights of
people whether singly or collectively.[8]

If that was not meant to sound the official death knell for
the abuse of secrecy in the Church, it came awfully close
by laying out—with the pope's own authority, remember—
sound antisecrecy principles as authoritative teaching.

Nuts and Bolts of an Open Meeting

As the future was to show, the turnout of seventy-five reporters in April 1972 for the bishops' first open meeting was on
the low side. The record-high number of credentialed media
people up to this time is seven hundred—a figure achieved
at the bishops' June 2002 assembly in Dallas, which came
at the height of the furor over clerical sex abuse and featured the bishops' adoption of a tough new national policy
on this grave problem. (The seven hundred included TV
and still photographers and technicians of various sorts, as
well as bona fide reporters.) In Dallas there was space for
only a handful of journalists in the bishops' meeting room;
the overflow—most of the crowd—was shunted off to a
hotel ballroom, where they followed the proceedings by
closed-circuit television on giant screens.

Dallas 2002 was unique in many ways, including in the
presence of so many media representatives. The press corps
that turns up for one of these assemblies usually totals a
hundred or so, with the actual number varying according
to the meeting agenda's supposed newsworthiness. The group
includes reporters for secular and religious news organizations (Associated Press, Catholic News Service, the *New*

[8] Ibid., nos. 120–21.

York Times, the *Washington Post*, the *Wanderer*, the *National Catholic Reporter*, *Our Sunday Visitor*, and other regulars). The Eternal Word Television Network (EWTN) films the open portions of the meeting from gavel to gavel, editing the footage for later broadcast while helpfully supplying a closed-circuit live feed to the press room. Other TV news organizations are free to cover the meeting and sometimes do, along with radio news and still photographers (the latter typically take their assigned shots, then leave). Occasionally a freelancer doing a magazine piece or researching a book turns up.

The system has served bishops and media well. Richard Ostling, writing in the early days, acknowledged the disadvantage for reporters arising from the need actually to *be there* to cover what was going on: "Instead of kibitzing over coffee in the press room or floating around town looking for other story ideas, reporters found themselves sitting through hours of canned reports and housekeeping items." On balance, though, open meetings were a plus. "Now [journalists] were able to size up the bishops as men, watch them interact, understand fully the context in which statements are made, and observe the full range of discussion, instead of depending on secondhand briefings and news releases after the fact."

But the big winners, Ostling concluded, were the bishops and, through them, the rest of the Church. "The bishops discovered that in this area ... they could be authentically Catholic and open in style, seem less aloof from their constituency, gain 'credibility,' and exhibit their own growing self-confidence as a body." [9] Not a bad payoff for opening some doors.

[9] Ostling, *Secrecy in the Church*, 43.

The Doors Start to Close Again

From the start, the bishops held onto—and regularly
exercised—the option of holding part of their general meeting in executive session. In practice, this turned out to mean
a single afternoon. The doors were shut, and the press and
observers had to find something else to do; for a few hours,
the bishops' deliberations were secret again. (At least, that
was the idea. Insiders—presumably, obliging bishops—
regularly leaked what happened in the executive session to
the press. If Acton and Veuillot had been living, they would
have appreciated that.)

To spend one afternoon in a meeting lasting three and a
half days (in November, that is; spring meetings are a bit
shorter) did not strike anyone as excessive. Quite possibly
the bishops had enough sensitive agenda items to warrant
this approach.

Somewhere along the way, things began to change. It is
hard to say exactly when, because at first no one knew a
change was occurring. I left the bishops' conference in 1987.
Beginning in the early 1990s, like a slow-moving solar eclipse,
the bishops' executive sessions little by little began chewing
up an increasing amount of meeting time. There were occasional remissions, but eventually a pattern emerged: for reasons unknown, the doors of the meeting room stayed shut
longer and longer.[10]

---

[10] At the bishops' general meeting in Los Angeles in June 2006, they spent
two days out of the three in closed sessions. In November 2006, the first two
days of the meeting were open and the next day and a half was closed. Of
the twenty-two hours of meeting time in November 2007, fourteen hours
were in open sessions and eight hours were closed, including four hours of
executive session, three hours devoted to "Prayer, Reflection, and Holy Hour",
and one hour for regional meetings.

One partial explanation may be that in the early years the hierarchy was still struggling to keep the lid on clerical sex abuse. In other cases, though, the secretiveness seemed to make no sense at all. A couple of years *after* the scandal erupted in 2002, for instance, the bishops spent most of their spring meeting discussing the pros and cons of having a high-level decision-making conference called a plenary council in an attempt to get the Church in the United States back on track. Prominent bishops delivered serious papers on issues in contemporary American Catholicism, and the presentations were followed by extended discussion. People who were present for the event said it showed the American hierarchy at its best—informed, engaged, deeply concerned about people's well-being; if Catholics could have seen and heard their bishops, it was said, they would have been edified and impressed. But Catholics *did not and could not see and hear their bishops* because, for unexplained reasons, this discussion was held behind closed doors. A valuable opportunity to refurbish the bishops' image and offer encouragement to worried Catholics was squandered for secrecy's sake.[11]

The new closed-door policy was fully in control by the time the bishops met in Washington in November 2005. Sixty percent of that assembly was in closed sessions. Before the press corps was tossed out, I asked several bishops what they'd be talking about.

"I have no idea", one said with a disgusted shrug. "They don't tell us in advance." It appeared that "they" were the officers of the bishops' conference and/or its forty-nine-member administrative committee.

[11] The papers from this meeting later were published in the Catholic News Service documentation periodical, *Origins*. Their appearance in this low-circulation publication, though welcome, was no substitute for the coverage they could have received from media at the time of their delivery.

A second bishop was more vociferous. He did not know what the executive session agenda was either. "And the trouble is," he added, clearly annoyed, "you don't get any documentation in advance, so there's no way you can prepare."

A third appeared somewhat more in the know about what was going on but no happier about it. Noting that the bishops a short time earlier had discussed—in open session—proposed new English translations for sections of the Mass, he said: "Before the meeting it was nip and tuck whether that discussion would be in executive session or not. Good grief—those are the *people's* parts of the Mass!"

Why the Doors Are Closed

As the doors of the bishops' meeting started staying closed longer and longer, I began now and then to write about what was happening and warn of the potential consequences. An official of the bishops' conference who shared my concerns asked me to make a presentation to the committee on communication of the United States Conference of Catholic Bishops (USCCB). "I'm just staff," he explained, "and they don't pay attention to me. Maybe they'll listen to you."

So, one day several years ago I found myself in the cavernous ground-floor conference room at USCCB headquarters in northeast Washington, D.C., sitting at the head of a very long oval table and facing a dozen or so bishops near the front and, farther off, a scattering of committee consultants and communication staff. The consultants and staff took no part in the dialogue that followed.

After a courteous introduction by the bishop-chairman, I made my case. The bishops had been down this same road—having secret meetings—many years before, and it had not worked then; there was every reason to suppose it would not work now either; documents of the Church like the Pastoral Instruction on Social Communications strongly discouraged unnecessary secrecy in the conduct of Church business; this was not only for pragmatic, self-interested reasons but because of the Second Vatican Council's vision of the Church as a communion—a community of faith with a hierarchical structure, to be sure, but also one in which all members possessed fundamental equality in dignity and rights, including the right to be treated as adults and permitted to know what was going on.

The bishops listened politely, but they did not yield an inch. Their arguments against openness were ones I had heard before. No matter who is making the case, it usually boils down to three considerations.

First, bishops use executive sessions to hear reports and engage in deliberations about pending business between them and Rome. The Holy See would be surprised and angry to have such matters discussed in public.

The answer to that is: sometimes yes, sometimes no. When very sensitive matters are being negotiated with the Vatican, closed discussions by the bishops may be the only responsible way for them to proceed. On the other hand, not every topic is all that sensitive: in fact, as matters stand, the bishops sometimes discuss issues outstanding between them and Rome in open session, and the heavens do not fall. It looks very much as if the decision to close the doors on these particular grounds was more or less arbitrary. The main result of secrecy then is to leave the Catholic people in the dark about matters that affect them at least as much as they do the American hierarchy and the Roman Curia.

Second, some matters are so painful that they have to be discussed in executive session, lest scandal result.

Clergy sex abuse is the obvious example. But, as the bishop quoted at the start of this book put it in his letter to me: "The attempt to keep such matters secret on grounds of protecting reputations ... simply allowed the evil to fester and grow. And when the dam of secrecy finally broke—as it always will—the whole Church suffered for its lack of candor."

Third, bishops speak to one another more openly when no one else is listening. Very likely that is so; but it is not much of an argument for secrecy when bishops are discussing matters important to the whole Church at an ordinary business meeting of the hierarchy.

There are several reasons for saying that. In lieu of a business meeting, the American bishops every three or four years have an extended, retreat-like, bishops-only assembly for prayer and reflection. No observers or press are allowed. The bishops have done that for years, and the custom seems to serve them well. No one objects. But there is no compelling reason to extend the closed-door policy to sessions of business meetings where it is not really needed.

Furthermore, this is not the only opportunity available to the bishops for off-the-record discussions. Most of them serve on one or more committees of the USCCB, and these meet in closed, confidential sessions several times a year. All of the bishops have regular opportunities to attend regional and provincial meetings with their colleagues and peers. Events like episcopal ordinations, funerals, anniversaries, and other special occasions bring bishops together for fellowship and conversation year-round. Surely that should be enough bishops-only gatherings in ordinary circumstances.

Finally, it is important to ask which is more important— that bishops multiply their opportunities for unbuttoned conversation with one another or that they go out of their way

to be open with the people they serve? Openness in conducting business that impacts on the People of God is a
central part of effective and transparent episcopal leadership. Taking stands on issues in public, then taking the flak
that comes from it, is part of being a leader today, in the
Church as much as anywhere else.

The Media and the Crisis

The sex abuse scandal not only has caused a crisis in the
internal communications of the Church (to be examined in
the next chapter), but it also has helped bring about a crisis
in the Church's media relations. The two crises interact and
reinforce each other.

As the story spread from Boston to the rest of the country in early 2002, journalists obsessively repeated the man-
tra that bishops had engaged in a "cover-up" of abusive
behavior by priests. To a considerable extent, the journalists were right.[12]

The bishops reaped the bitter fruits of secrecy at their
meeting in Dallas, Texas, in June 2002. The press in Dallas
clearly were of one mind that the Catholic hierarchy was
getting its well-deserved comeuppance. They were glad to
record the event. I covered that surreal meeting as a reporter,

[12] But not as right as is widely believed. A former director of communications for the United States Conference of Catholic Bishops points out that
research by the John Jay College of Criminal Justice on the scope of abuse
by Catholic clergy from 1950 through 2002 found that by 1990 only 17
percent of the abuse cases now known to have occurred had been reported
to the dioceses. Cover-ups certainly took place; but bishops cannot reasonably be accused of covering up what they didn't know about. Whether they
might have known and should have known are, of course, other questions.
Cf. Msgr. Francis J. Maniscalco, "A Missing Chapter in the Sexual Abuse
Crisis", *Priest*, April 2006.

and something I wrote at the time captures a bit of the special aura of this public flaying:

> To a marked degree, the Dallas assembly was about feelings.
>
> As the bishops began a closed-door session the first afternoon, their presiding officer invited them to share feelings.
>
> "So I had to sit there and listen to feelings," a bishop recounting the episode snorted.
>
> "Did you hold hands?" one of his listeners asked. . . .
>
> Members of the media swarm shared insights of their own. Noting that protestors planned a candlelight vigil outside while the bishops celebrated Mass, one assured another, "That's the news—outside."
>
> Like many of his colleagues, he was missing the point. The news in Dallas was what was happening inside—inside the bishops' heads and hearts.
>
> In the end, they approved a policy that, among other things, requires the dismissal from priestly ministry even of elderly priests who might have committed only one misdeed, many years before, and have served with distinction since then. Abuse victims and the media demanded "zero tolerance" and the bishops gave it to them, in very nearly its toughest form. . . .
>
> While coming down like a ton of bricks on elderly clerics, the bishops shied away from looking at the causes of the dreadful mess—nasty things like homosexuality among priests, theological rationalizing on the subject of sex, and the entrenched self-protectiveness of the old clericalist culture. . . .
>
> It was obvious that the bishops are sick of taking the heat. In still another outburst of feeling, Bishop Wilton Gregory of Belleville, Ill. [now archbishop of Atlanta], their president, lit into the media, calling some coverage of the scandal "hysterical" and complaining that the bishops' image had been "distorted" by the press.

> The bishops' response was, in part at least, to get tough with elderly priests who did something very wrong a long time ago but repented and got on with their lives.
>
> The morning after the bishops' 239–13 vote, one observer tapped the banner headline in *The Dallas Morning News*—"Bishops Adopt Abuse Policy"—and said to another, "It should read, 'They Did What We Told Them To Do.' " [13]

Much earlier, I had seen it all taking shape, though I had not realized it at the time. The problem of sex abuse of minors by Catholic priests first came to public attention in 1984, when a priest named Gilbert Gauthé went on trial on sexual molestation charges in Lafayette, Louisiana. Like most other people, I supposed this was a rare, isolated case. At the time, I was information director of the bishops' conference in Washington, a member of the general secretary's staff, and there was little that I did not know about the organization's affairs. But clergy sex abuse was different. I was kept studiously, consistently, in the dark. Speaking to one another in my presence, priests on the general secretariat staff made occasional, oblique remarks that hinted at a problem that might be somewhat larger than a single, isolated case, but they said nothing to open up the secret to me.

That state of affairs persisted until late 1987, when I left to take another job. At no time from the start of the Gauthé trial in 1984 to my departure in 1987 did anyone in a responsible position inform me of the nature and magnitude of the problem or seek my professional advice as a communicator.

At least three factors were at work to account for that. One was the desire of conscientious clergymen not to give

[13] Russell Shaw, "'Zero Tolerance' wins as Bishops take a Hard Line," *Our Sunday Visitor*, June 30, 2002.

scandal to a layman concerning serious misbehavior by priests. The second was fear that sharing this information with the conference's chief information officer risked having it end up in the hands of the press. (True, for many years I had been trusted with confidential information of all kinds, without that happening; but in the eyes of the priests with whom I worked, clergy sex abuse was too sensitive to take the risk.) Finally, I conclude with regret that my colleagues, desperate to protect the reputation of the priesthood, had fallen back on the clericalist culture's old tactic of circling the wagons when under attack.

The point is not that I would have come up with some brilliant strategy if I had been consulted. At the time, I probably would have agreed that silence and secrecy were best. But no one thought to speak with, or even inform, me or other Church communicators and get their advice. Lawyers, yes. Psychiatrists and psychologists, certainly. But communicators—definitely not. For the clericalist culture, secrecy was the only conceivable response to clergy sex abuse. And you do not need communicators to keep a secret, do you?

The Cost of Secrecy

As we know now, secrecy was a terrible mistake. It allowed a serious problem to become a disaster for abuse victims; for innocent priests who found themselves tarred with the same brush as their guilty brothers; for confused, frightened bishops; and eventually for the whole Church. The media feasted on it.

That feasting itself deserves more attention than it has generally gotten up to now. Consider that the incidence of sex abuse of children and young people may be greater, both absolutely and proportionately, among public school teachers than it is among Catholic priests; yet the media seldom say anything about that. The chancellor of the Denver archdiocese, a layman and father of four, writes of the "hypocrisy" of journalists and legislators who have pilloried the Church on this issue even as the same problem "pervades our public schools".[14]

Up to a point at least, things might have been different. To a great extent the bishops' hands were tied by the confidentiality of court proceedings and sealed settlements, as well as respect for the privacy rights of individuals, both victims and accused. But there also were constructive things that could have been done and were not.

In June 1992, for instance, the National Conference of Catholic Bishops adopted a set of "five principles" for dioceses to follow in dealing with the problem. The principles included responding promptly to allegations, suspending any cleric or Church employee who was credibly accused, complying with civil law and cooperating with the authorities, engaging in outreach to victims, and generally committing to handle the issue "as openly as possible". Next year the bishops' conference created an ad hoc committee to monitor the situation.

These steps were all to the good. Unfortunately, though, acceptance of the principles was voluntary for dioceses. As we now know, the incidence of clergy sex abuse had peaked

---

[14] Francis X. Maier, "Shakedown: How Catholics Are Getting Ripped Off in the Name of Justice", *Crisis*, May 2006. An investigation by the Associated Press found that from 2001 through 2005, 270 public school educators in the United States were known to have had their teaching credentials revoked or denied, or had surrendered them or were otherwise sanctioned following charges of misconduct. Most such abuse "never gets reported", the news agency said. (Associated Press, "Sexual Misconduct Plagues Public Schools", October 21, 2007, AOL News.)

in the 1970s and had been declining since then;[15] the drop-off apparently accelerated in dioceses that accepted and implemented the principles. Yet information like that was generally unavailable to the public, and this dearth of hard facts created an information vacuum that the crisis of 2002 often would fill with sensationalism and exaggeration.

Even after the story of abuse and cover-up in Boston broke in January 2002 in the *Boston Globe*, the conference of bishops could say or do almost nothing about it in the crucial early weeks. For one thing, over the years the national organization hadn't collected comprehensive data on the problem—data that, if available at this critical moment and promptly released, would have countered the speculation that suggested a veritable epidemic of abuse was still occurring. As it was, wildly inflated estimates of the number of victims and abusive priests were allowed to circulate uncontested.

The bishops' conference also was obliged to keep hands off at first for reasons of ecclesiology. The crisis was viewed as "Boston's problem", and the beleaguered Archdiocese of Boston was left alone to deal with the situation as best it could. This was disastrously naïve. From the very start, the disclosures in Boston were a national story, not a local one, and they had an escalating impact on the Catholic Church throughout the United States. An ancient ecclesiological model

---

[15] The National Review Board in 2004 reported that 4,392 priests in the United States were accused of sexually abusing approximately 10,667 minors between 1950 and 2002. That was approximately 4% of the total number of active priests in that time. Broken down by decade, 9.7% of the reported cases of abuse began in the 1950s, 26.1% in the 1960s, 35.5% in the 1970s, 22.6% in the 1980s, and 6.2% between 1990 and 2002 (*The Causes and Context of the Clergy Sexual Abuse of Minors Crisis* [Washington, D.C.: United States Conference of Catholic Bishops, 2004]). These numbers have continued to rise, though at a decelerating pace, as additional incidents of newly reported abuse in the past have been noted in annual reports.

of autonomous "local churches" and their bishops, existing in isolation from one another, was applied to the world of contemporary mass media where it surely did not fit.

Eventually this thinking broke down as media ferreted out tales of abuse and cover-up in other dioceses far removed from Boston. But this ecclesiology coming out of a very different time and place already had condemned the Church in America to an extended period of unresisted pummeling at the hands of journalists at a moment when a swift response was desperately needed.

Summing up the costs of secrecy in this crisis, journalist Peter Steinfels concludes that even after serious reform efforts by the bishops at the national level had begun in the early 1990s, the hierarchy continued to pass up opportunities for getting the facts out.

> With few exceptions, they did not report publicly how many priests had been accused, pressured out of the active priesthood, sent into treatment, or returned to supervised assignments if the treatment centers so advised. Bishops did not, in fact, explain clearly and publicly what state-of-the-art therapy was then telling them about treatment and recidivism, and what treatment and reassignment policies they were following. Nor did they reveal the number of settlements, quite apart from any further details, or how much money had gone into them and into treatment. In far too many cases, the bishops did not reveal to pastors or other supervisors the history of priests being reassigned after treatment.

Sometimes the silence resulted from "considerations of confidentiality", Steinfels says, and sometimes from the "naïve assumption" that Catholics had closely followed the news coverage of individual abuse cases and kept the details in mind. But on the whole, something else was at work.

[S]haring information of this sort did not come naturally to bishops. Most of this failure to disclose—indeed aggressively to inform and educate Catholics about—the sex abuse scandals revealed after 1985 almost certainly sprang from deeply ingrained habits of holding information within a very narrow circle of advisers and decision-makers. In 2002 the church would pay dearly for this failure.[16]

The Church is still paying for it today and will continue to pay for years to come.

[16] Peter Steinfels, *A People Adrift* (New York: Simon and Schuster, 2003), 59.

Chapter Four

ALL IN THE FAMILY?

Good news. It is said that American bishops have gotten better at dealing with the press since the clergy sex abuse scandal broke. Granted, among the sources of the judgment that some are "more media savvy" than they used to be are "media specialists who advise the bishops", who have a vested interest in discerning progress in their pupils; but anyway, it is encouraging if true. For the Church's leaders to be at ease talking with journalists is in the Church's best interests as well as their own.[1]

Without wanting to rain on anybody's parade, though, I think another point also needs to be made. Knowing how to give an interview or handle yourself in a news conference, important though it is for bishops and others in public positions of leadership, is a teachable technical skill, on the order of whistling, that leaves matters of substance untouched. It is also a skill often abused by demagogues and charlatans both in and out of the religious world.

And—something especially relevant here—it has very little to do with responsible internal communication in the Church.

[1] See Tom Carney, "Crisis Leads to More Media Savvy", *National Catholic Reporter*, July 14, 2006.

The abuse of secrecy in external communications often has poisoned the Church's relationship with the media and defaced her image in the eyes of the world. Sometimes, as in the sex abuse scandal, this has happened on a horrendous scale. More subtle, but possibly even more destructive in the long run, is the silent damage done by secrecy and its cousins—stonewalling, happy talk, deception, failure to consult, the de facto suppression of public opinion, the rejection of accountability, the repudiation of shared responsibility on clericalist grounds—to the internal life of the Church. Failures of internal communication like these would be serious matters in any institution or organization, because they sap morale, weaken solidarity, and create a blend of apathy and alienation that undermines the group's capacity for effective action in propagating and defending its values and beliefs. In the case of the Church, the failures not only have these bad results but strike at the Church's self-understanding as a community of faith, the People of God, the body of Christ.

Some Examples

Most Catholics can cite instances of the failure of internal communication from their own experience of belonging to the Church.

Suffering from declining numbers and strapped for cash to support its elderly, retired members, a women's religious community kept mum while negotiating the sale of the popular Catholic girls' school it had operated in an East Coast diocese for many years. When the deal was done and the news finally came out, lay teachers, students, and parents were thunderstruck to learn that they had been left high and dry by the sisters, who had not breathed a word about what was going on. When confronted by angry people who had trusted them, the sisters said they had kept quiet for fear of spoiling the deal.

Here is an incident that manages to combine deception with stonewalling.

A layman got a mailing from a men's religious order advertising a drawing with a prize of several thousand dollars. "You Have Won!" announced a large headline on the letter's first page. The text seemed to confirm that good news. All the lucky winner needed to do to get his money was fill out and return a form on which the winning number—assigned only to him—was printed. No payment was required, the letter assured him, although donations to the order to support its numerous good works would of course be gratefully received.

Pleased but skeptical, this layman took the precaution of examining the fine print on the back of the letter. The verbiage was murky, but the message came through anyway: the person receiving this letter would have won the drawing *if, and only if*, the preprinted number on the entry form turned out to be the winning number in the drawing.

Angered by this clumsy attempt at deception, the layman wrote to the priest whose printed signature was on the letter. He pointed out that many good, gullible souls would be taken in by this scam and, along with returning the form with the "winning" number, would tuck a check for five or ten dollars in the envelope to express their gratitude to the religious order that was the source of this windfall. Considering all the other problems the Church had these days, the man wrote, surely she did not also need to have a religious community involved in a shoddy con game like this.

The layman got no reply.

And here is an instance of brazen lying.

A reporter called the information director of a Catholic group that lately had begun to make its annual budget public. The numbers do not add up, the reporter said. Expenses are a lot more than revenue, and there is no indication of how the shortfall is going to be covered.

The information director took the query to the organization's finance director, a Catholic layman who had served the Church with distinction in various capacities for many years. The finance director responded with an explanation that involved things like carryovers and nonreportable assets. The information director did not understand a word, but, trusting his source, he dutifully took the answer back to the reporter. The journalist was unpersuaded but chose not to pursue the matter.

Only later did the information director find out that the finance director had told him a cock-and-bull story. The truth was that the group had income from investments that, for whatever reason or reasons, it did not care to publicize. Since the finance director's clerical superiors had not authorized him to say anything about that, he handled the unwanted question by the simple device of lying. Mulling that over, the information director told himself, "I suppose the poor guy reasoned that if the clergy in charge here wanted him to hush this up, there couldn't be anything wrong with lying. Just doing what Father told him, after all."

Father John Beal, a canon lawyer at the Catholic University of America, calls the related rights of information and expression in the Church "conspicuous casualties" of the sex abuse scandal. Along with the fallout from that crisis, however, he sees at work a "deeply ingrained bias" on the part of Church authorities, making it "impossible for the law [of the Church] and those who administer it to recognize any genuine equality between the ordinary faithful and their ordained leaders or, at least, to give the recognition of such equality any practical effect." Father Beal writes:

> During the current crisis, the utter disregard for the rights of the faithful to information and expression betrays the chronic inability of church authorities to see and treat the faithful (including most of the so-called "lower clergy") as anything but ignorant children, an inability fostered and reinforced by a legal system that continues to structure the church as a society of unequals, despite pious protestations to the contrary.[2]

It seems that we have a problem.

In the spring of 2006, as noted earlier, the Archdiocese of Boston, hard pressed financially, published a comprehensive financial report showing a $46 million operating deficit. The audited report was widely praised as a model for other dioceses because of its accuracy, scope, and detail. "This is what Catholics around the country are going to start expecting", an observer was quoted as saying. It takes nothing away from Boston's bold and creative move, however, to point out that the archdiocese turned to full financial disclosure only after it found itself with a desperate situation on its hands.

And elsewhere? It is far from clear that Boston will be a model; for, as one archbishop remarked, "Explaining all of the financial operations of a diocese in a way that's easy for the average person to understand is more complicated than

---

[2] John Beal, "It Shall Not Be So among You!" in *Governance, Accountability, and the Future of the Catholic Church*, ed. Francis Oakley and Bruce Russett (New York: Continuum, 2004), 91–92.

it sounds. It is easy for the data to get misinterpreted." [3] This is a variation on a familiar theme: "If we tell them the truth, they won't understand. So let's tell them a little less than the truth." As Orestes Brownson and John Henry Newman pointed out a century and a half ago, perpetuating the ignorance of the laity is a self-defeating strategy for the Church.

The Importance of Public Opinion

Official statements of the Church about public opinion, internal communication, and related matters carry a strong, positive message.

That is so, for instance, with *Il Rapido Sviluppo* (Rapid Development), the apostolic letter that was the last major public document issued by Pope John Paul II. Dated January 24, 2005—just a little over two months before his death—it deals mainly with the media and the Church's external communications, but it also contains a fairly substantial discussion of internal communication.

Recalling Pope Pius XII's famous words about the need for public opinion in the Church, and extending his own blessing to an internal dialogue among Catholics that is "respectful of justice and prudence", John Paul writes that communication should "tend towards a constructive dialogue, so as to promote a correctly-informed and discerning public opinion within the Christian community". And he quotes Vatican Council II:

> A great many wonderful things are to be hoped for from this familiar dialogue between the laity and their spiritual

[3] Emily Stimpson, "Seeking to Restore Trust, Boston Discloses Finances", *Our Sunday Visitor*, May 21, 2006.

leaders: in the laity a strengthened sense of personal responsibility; a renewed enthusiasm; a more ready application of their talents to the projects of their spiritual leaders. The latter, on the other hand, aided by the experience of the laity, can more clearly and more incisively come to decisions regarding both spiritual and temporal matters. In this way, the whole Church, strengthened by each one of its members, may more effectively fulfill its mission for the life of the world.[4]

Pope John Paul might also have quoted this well-known statement of the Council regarding internal communication:

To [the pastors of the Church] the laity should disclose their needs and desires with that liberty and confidence which befits children of God and brothers of Christ. By reason of the knowledge, competence or preeminence which they have the laity are empowered—indeed sometimes obliged—to manifest their opinion on those things which pertain to the good of the Church. If the occasion should arise this should be done through the institutions established by the Church for that purpose.[5]

As we saw earlier, *Communio et Progressio*, the pastoral instruction published by the Vatican's Commission for Social Communications in 1971, contains a very strong and explicit endorsement of public opinion, two-way communication, and access to information in the Church.[6] Words of approval

[4] Pope John Paul II, apostolic letter *Il Rapido Sviluppo* (Rapid Development) (January 24, 2005), no. 12. The quotation is from Vatican Council II, Dogmatic Constitution on the Church, *Lumen Gentium* (November 21, 1964), no. 37.

[5] *Lumen Gentium*, no. 37.

[6] See Pontifical Commission for Social Communications, Pastoral Instruction on the Means of Social Communication, *Communio et Progressio* (May 23, 1971), nos. 114–21.

for public opinion even found their way into the 1983 Code
of Canon Law, in language drawn largely from the Council:

> The Christian faithful are free to make known their needs,
> especially spiritual ones, and their desires to the pastors of
> the Church.
>
> In accord with the knowledge, competence and preemi-
> nence which they possess, they have the right and even at times
> a duty to manifest to the sacred pastors their opinion on mat-
> ters which pertain to the good of the Church, and they have
> a right to make their opinions known to the other Christian
> faithful, with due regard for the integrity of faith and morals
> and reverence toward their pastors, and with consideration for
> the common good and the the dignity of persons.[7]

Also deserving of mention are documents published in 1992,
2000, and 2002 by the Vatican's Council (formerly Commission) for Social Communications and titled, respec-
tively, *Aetatis Novae* (A New Era), *Ethics in Communications*,
and *The Church and Internet*.

Aetatis Novae is a pastoral instruction marking the twentieth anniversary of the earlier pastoral instruction on communications, *Communio et Progressio*. Along with much else,
it affirms the need to "constantly ... recall the importance
of the fundamental right of dialogue and information within
the Church ... and to continue to seek effective means,
including a responsible use of media of social communications, for realizing and protecting this right." [8]

Picking up on this thought, *Ethics in Communications*
declares: "A two-way flow of information and views between
pastors and faithful, freedom of expression sensitive to the

[7] Canon 212.2, 212.3.

[8] Pastoral Instruction on Social Communications on the Twentieth Anniversary of *Communio et Progressio*, *Aetatis Novae* (February 22, 1992), no. 10.

well being of the community and to the role of the Magisterium in fostering it, and responsible public opinion are all important expressions of 'the fundamental right of dialogue and information within the Church.' " [9]

Particularly interesting is *The Church and Internet*, which displays a sophisticated and creative understanding of, and openness to, the potential of new technology in relation to internal communication, including exchanges of information, the development of public opinion, and participation in decision making. Noting that the interactivity which the Internet makes possible and easy represents a profound change from "the one-way, top-down communication of the past", the document says the Internet provides an "effective technological means of realizing [the] vision" sketched by previous Church documents regarding the Church's internal communications. Then it adds:

> Here, then, is an instrument that can be put creatively to use for various aspects of administration and governance. Along with opening up channels for the expression of public opinion, we have in mind such things as consulting experts, preparing meetings, and practicing collaboration in and among particular churches and religious institutes on local, national, and international levels. [10]

Reality vs. Ideal: The Catholic Press

On the whole, this adds up to a creditable record at the level of official statements, since the documents take a

[9] Pontifical Council for Social Communications, *Ethics in Communications* (June 4, 2000), no. 6.

[10] Pontifical Council for Social Communications, *The Church and Internet* (February 22, 2002), no. 6.

commendably enlightened view of questions like two-way communication, openness in sharing information, public opinion, and a participatory approach to decision making. But the reality of internal communication in the Church by no means measures up to the ideal.

Take Vatican II's mention in *Lumen Gentium* of "the institutions established by the Church for that purpose"—i.e., to make it possible for lay people to tell the Church's leaders their views concerning the good of the Church. The question that naturally raises is: What institutions is *Lumen Gentium* talking about?

The Council does not say, but three possibilities come to mind: the Catholic press and now, by extension, Catholic Web sites, the mail (today including e-mail), and diocesan and parish councils. There are problems with all three.

Start with the Catholic press. At first glance, it seems well suited to be an instrument for the formation and expression of Catholic opinion so warmly commended by Vatican II. The 2007 figures from the Catholic Press Association of the United States and Canada show 195 U.S. Catholic newspapers with a combined circulation of nearly 6.5 million, 223 magazines with a circulation of nearly 13 million, 115 newsletters with a circulation of more than 4.1 million, and 34 U.S. Catholic foreign-language publications with circulation a little over 1 million. That is a total of 567 publications with combined circulation of about 24.3 million—an impressively large forum for a flourishing public opinion![11]

But the numbers are deceptive. Very many of these publications are technical journals or periodicals serving the needs

---

[11] Statistical Summary, *2007 Catholic Press Directory* (Ronkonkoma, N.Y.: Catholic Press Association, 2007), 4.

and interests of special groups (mission magazines, newsletters of Church-related institutions and organizations, and the like). At the national level, newspapers and magazines that can realistically be considered platforms for public opinion in the manner envisaged by Vatican II number only a handful—*Commonweal*, *America*, *Catholic World Report*, the *National Catholic Reporter*, the *Wanderer*, *Our Sunday Visitor*, the *National Catholic Register*, and a few others. Their combined circulation is fewer than three hundred thousand in an American Catholic population officially said to number over sixty-seven million.

Moreover, the national publications were not "established by the Church" for the purpose of fostering public opinion, as *Lumen Gentium* specifies. They were established at the initiative of lay people and religious orders that continue to publish them today; taken as a group, they do indeed reflect a striking range of opinion extending from far left to far right, but in no sense are they official or even semi-official organs through which rank-and-file Catholics are encouraged to express their views to the leadership. If the truth were told, in fact, the leadership regards several of the publications as distinct nuisances and would be pleased if they went out of business.

And the diocesan press? According to the Catholic Press Association, in 2007 there were 163 U.S. diocesan newspapers with a combined circulation of nearly six million. If American Catholicism possesses institutions "established by the Church" to promote a lively public opinion, then, surely, the casual observer might say, it is these official organs.

The casual observer would be wrong. There may be exceptions, but most diocesan papers simply do not give space to views that disagree with diocesan policy on anything of a serious nature. (The exceptions are news stories

and commentary that cite obviously hostile opinions in order
to refute them or warn readers against them.) Neither their
editors nor their bishop-publishers see it as their role to do
otherwise. Defending the diocesan press against the charge
of being "just a lap dog of the bishops", the president of
the Catholic Press Association at the time this is written
gives this account of the guiding philosophy of a diocesan
newspaper:

> Most diocesan publications are departments—and mini-
> stries—of the diocese. Usually, the bishop-publisher views
> his role as publisher from the perspective of his larger role,
> as chief shepherd of the diocese.... We should not be
> ashamed of letting our readers know that we write articles
> from a certain objective.... We have the perspective of tell-
> ing of God's great love for humanity.... While some might
> wish for diocesan publications to become great sources of
> debate on hot church topics, most of our readers are more
> concerned about how to make sure their kids don't access
> porn on the Internet, how to make sense out of the new
> Medicare plans for their parents and grandparents, and if
> their job is going to be outsourced overseas. The decline in
> the number of priests in the United States just isn't some-
> thing that keeps them awake at night.[12]

While that is a narrow vision of what a diocesan newspaper
exists to do, it is a realistic one and in some ways not
unattractive. Who could be so meanspirited, after all, as to
wish readers of the Catholic press to lose sleep over a little
thing like the steep decline in the number of Catholic priests
now occurring in the United States? Still, one thing diocesan newspapers definitely are *not*, as this spokesperson for

[12] Helen Osman, "One-Two Punch of Criticism Hits Diocesan Press",
Catholic Journalist, December 2005.

the Catholic press makes clear, is institutions engaged in nurturing public opinion and the "familiar dialogue between the laity and their spiritual leaders" of which Vatican Council II spoke.

Internet weblogs—"blogs"—are a relatively new presence on this scene. The blogs are lively, entertaining, sometimes informative, and nothing if not provocatively opinionated. They provide a continuous medley of undifferentiated fact, fantasy, and unfiltered rumor and speculation, along with outrageous ego-tripping by their proprietors and users.

But their value as forums for the exchange of opinion is very questionable. Like talks to like in the blogosphere: conservatives post on conservative blogs, liberals on liberal ones. Bloggers receive reinforcement of the views they already hold; there is little real incentive for them to think anything new.

Love them or hate them, Catholic blogs, like blogs in general, are a permanent addition to the Areopagus of our times (as Pope John Paul famously called the media). Serious analysis is overdue of this new vehicle for Catholics to express their opinions. Clearly, the blogs of Catholic interest are unofficial by definition—hardly the "institutions" envisaged by Vatican II for stimulating healthy public opinion. Cumulatively, they contribute to the polarization in the Church.

It is conventional wisdom that blogs have changed politics and journalism, and very likely they have. Probably they have begun also to change decision making in the Church, although changes there are likely to be slower than most other places, given the Church's resistance to structural change. Whether this will be for good or ill cannot be predicted. The anarchic populism of the blogosphere is heady and potentially dangerous.

The structural checks and balances of traditional journalism are totally lacking in this realm. Every blogger is free to say very nearly whatever he wants, which often means questioning the motives of ideological opponents and calling them names. This is hardly a healthy influence on the process of governing the Church. Blogging may be cathartic for the bloggers, but it is not particularly helpful for anyone else.

Official Church-sponsored websites range from mediocre to excellent. Many perform a useful service. The Vatican website (www.vatican.va), for example, offers ready access to the texts of official documents, as well as useful background information. But the official sites also are buttoned-down purveyors of approved news and views. As such, they are electronic examples of old-fashioned, top-down, one-way communication. Seldom do they provide opportunity for interactivity. Their unintended message is: "We will tell you what you need to know. What you think about it is of no concern to us." That makes them Internet versions of the house organ Catholic press.

Writing Letters

If the diocesan newspaper and diocesan website turn out not to be very promising vehicles of public opinion, Catholic lay people at least have the option of writing letters to Church leaders. Many do. But as most people who've written a few such letters can attest, the results tend to be mixed. Respectful, well-reasoned letters to bishops, pastors, and others in leadership positions sometimes receive respectful, well-reasoned replies. But in other cases the response is a form letter ("Thank you for sharing your opinion . . ."), while in some cases there's no response at all.

Here are two instances of that.

An alumnus of a prominent Catholic university came across an interview with his school's priest-president in an academic journal in which the president remarked that certain practices in the celebration of the liturgy on his campus were designed to pave the way for the day when women would be ordained as priests in the Catholic Church. Slightly taken aback, the alumnus wrote the president a polite letter expressing the view that this was a somewhat questionable stance for a university that advertised itself as operating in the Catholic tradition. He got no reply.

Again: a layman observed a fairly serious liturgical abuse in the celebration of Mass in his parish. He wrote the pastor a respectful letter calling attention to what was happening and enclosed a photocopy of the relevant section of the General Instruction of the Roman Missal, the normative Church document on such matters. He got no reply. After several weeks of silence, he wrote the pastor again, respectfully noting that his first letter might have been lost in the mail, repeating his original point, and enclosing the same documentation. He got no reply. The pastor often saw this man in and around church, and the two now and then exchanged a few words, but the pastor said nothing about the letters. The liturgical abuse continued.

After many months had passed, the parish's pastoral associate met the layman leaving church after Mass. "We're going to start doing it your way", she cheerfully announced. And soon the parish did. The liturgical abuse vanished. The layman wondered if the local chancery had sent pastors a notice about the practice in question, but he had no way of knowing if that was so. The pastor to this day has not breathed a word about the two letters.

These are two small incidents. But are they rare? Many Catholics have similar stories to tell. Writing letters to the bishop or the pastor is a legitimate exercise of the right of public opinion in the Church; sometimes it may even get results. But all too often even the most intelligent, polite, and well-reasoned letters are ignored by people in positions of authority who evidently feel they are not answerable to the people of the Church.

The problem here is not just rudeness, although the behavior described certainly is rude. Much more important, rudeness like this contradicts the ideal of interpersonal relationships grounded in Christ; it is an offense against Church communion.

Spin and Happy Talk

Another major obstacle to internal communication in the Church is the persistence of ecclesiastical spin. Often this reflects the well-intentioned but paternalistic mindset of persons in official positions who, if truth were told, consider lay people unqualified to participate in serious discussions of Church issues and have no interest in supplying them with information and ideas to bring them up to speed. Instead of engaging in candid communication, they engage in spin.

The advantages of spin have been recognized for many years. The journalist and counselor of presidents Walter Lippmann, a quintessential specimen of the American public policy elite, set forth the rationale in 1922 in his book *Public Opinion*. Many issues of the present day, he argued, are simply too complex for the leaders of democracies to explain to the public in order to win people's assent for the leaders' preferred approaches. The solution lay instead in what

Lippmann called "the manufacture of consent". Opportunities for what he conceded was a form of "manipulation" were "open to anyone who understands the process".

Manufacturing consent was not new, Lippmann contended, but the techniques of doing it had become vastly more sophisticated in modern times "because it is now based on analysis rather than on rule of thumb. . . . [A]s a result of psychological research, coupled with the modern means of communication, the practice of democracy has turned a corner [and] persuasion has become a self-conscious and a regular organ of popular government." [13]

Looking back to the 1920s from the vantage point of an era in which subtle means for massaging popular opinion have become commonplace—an era, furthermore, entirely too familiar for comfort with propaganda (in what Lippman called "the sinister meaning of the word")—these remarks carry disturbing implications for political society. But does the manufacturing of consent also occur in the world of religion? Leaving aside the occasional cult leader who practices mind control over his deluded followers, are not most religious leaders too decent to attempt such a thing?

Perhaps so. But it does not follow that religious leaders are not influenced by the example of no-holds-barred practitioners of spin and manipulation in the worlds of politics and commerce—and even some of their less scrupulous brethren in religion. And although churches may usually lack the expensive tools of manipulation that advertisers and political campaign consultants possess, religion has practiced its own kinds of spin for a long time.

---

[13] Walter Lippmann, *Public Opinion* (New York: Free Press Paperbacks, 1997), 158.

Newman spoke bitingly about one of these in the 1830s
in a sermon called "The Religion of the Day". "Every thing
is bright and cheerful. Religion is pleasant and easy; benev-
olence is the chief virtue; intolerance, bigotry, excess of
zeal, are the first of sins. Austerity is an absurdity;—even
firmness is looked on with an unfriendly, suspicious eye."
In these circumstances, Newman remarked, people grow
hostile to what is old in religion and become eager for the
new—"dissatisfied with things as they are, desirous of a
change *as such*, as if alteration itself must be a relief".[14]
Anybody who lived through the postconciliar era in American Catholicism extending from the late 1960s until well
into the 1980s (and, some would argue, continuing to this
very day) is well acquainted with the mentality. One form
in which it found—and continues to find—expression is an
ecclesiastical version of spin that years ago I took to calling
"happy talk".

Happy talk is central to the rhetoric of religious people,
leaders and ordinary Catholics alike, who are accustomed
to dismiss signs of crisis and decline in the Church as matters of little importance, painful at the time perhaps but
somehow beneficial in the long run. This was how bishops
and pastors of the 1970s and 1980s routinely reacted when
confronted with hard evidence that attendance at Sunday
(or Saturday evening) Mass had been falling since the 1960s
and was continuing to decline.[15]

---

[14] John Henry Newman, "The Religion of the Day", in *Parochial and Plain
Sermons* (San Francisco: Ignatius Press, 1987), 198.

[15] The numbers cited vary according to the methodology used to obtain
them. In general terms, in the mid-1960s about two American Catholics out
of three went to Mass on any given Sunday; now it is about one out of
three—and less in some places. The rate of Mass attendance in the United
States nevertheless is a great deal higher than it is in much of western Europe.

Although in many cases the happy-talkers of those years have sobered up on this subject by now, the old happy talk can sometimes still be heard, as in the following: "Participation in the liturgy is a common means of spiritual formation. Though weekly Mass attendance has declined ... laity are participating in worship more extensively and in greater depth through the ministerial roles of reading, singing, distributing communion, assisting at the altar, providing hospitality and so on." [16] But *are* the fewer who go to Mass these days also participating better? How can anyone pretend to know? There is no empirical evidence that "reading, singing, distributing communion", and the other activities enumerated signify more devout, prayerful participation in the Eucharist than the less demonstrative presence of congregations at Mass did in years gone by. All that can be said for certain is that they involve more visible and audible activity by a few.

Similar unreality now prevails in many other areas of American Catholic life and on many other issues—the Catholic identity of Catholic colleges and universities, the effectiveness of religious education, and the acceptance of the teaching authority of the Church, to mention just a few. Unreality is probably most pronounced, and most studiously ignored, on the subject of sex, especially contraception. With a few exceptions, when it comes to sex, priests do not speak the truth to the laity, laity do not speak the truth to priests, and bishops seldom speak the truth to either group or have the truth spoken to them.

---

[16] H. Richard McCord Jr., "Full, Conscious, and Active Participation: The Laity's Quest", in *The Continuing Agenda*, ed. Anthony J. Cernera (Fairfield, Conn.: Sacred Heart University Press, 1997), 160. McCord currently is director of the laity office of the United States Conference of Catholic Bishops.

Although the Vatican says people are entitled to kneel down
to receive communion if they wish, bishops and pastors have
been known to rebuke those who do; but rarely does a bishop
or pastor speak out against the sin of contraception or adul-
tery or cohabitation, or chastise a pro-choice Catholic pol-
itician who insists he has the right to receive communion.
Corrosive unreality and a conspiracy of silence are widespread on matters like these; and the significant differences
that exist, from diocese to diocese and parish to parish,
heighten the impression that a dictatorship of relativism not
unlike the one decried by Pope Benedict XVI in his famous
talk to the cardinals on the eve of the conclave that elected
him pope has gained more than a small foothold in the Church.

Even the sex abuse crisis produces instances of happy talk
and spin.

An editorial in the *National Catholic Reporter* discounts
the thought that sexual abuse of minors by priests was "a
gay thing".[17] Yet the figures cited by the newspaper itself
show that the victims of clergy sex abuse were, by an over-
whelming margin, boys; and the National Review Board's
landmark "causes and context" report speaks of the "homosexual behavior that characterized the vast majority of the
cases of abuse observed in recent decades". That 81 percent
of the reported victims were boys "shows that the crisis
was characterized by homosexual behavior", the Review
Board says.[18] Ironically, the *Catholic Reporter* editorial is
headed "Spin without End in Abuse Scandal".

Or consider the bishop of a Southwestern diocese who
moved a notorious abuser-priest from parish to parish instead

[17] Editorial, *National Catholic Reporter*, June 16, 2006.
[18] National Review Board, "Report: Causes and Context of the Sexual
Abuse Crisis", *Origins*, March 11, 2004.

of taking steps to halt the priest's career. The priest's crimes did untold damage to victims and ended up costing the diocese many millions of dollars in settlements. As the bishop approached the mandatory retirement age of seventy-five, his diocesan newspaper asked him what he would do differently if he could. His answer: he would do more to encourage well-to-do people to be generous to the poor. Happy talk by omission, you might say.

Happy talk and its equivalents are by no means as trivial as at first they may seem. Implicitly, these distortions and denials of reality confer legitimacy upon abusive and destructive practices that should be rooted out, not papered over. They undermine the truthfulness and openness that are essential to communion in the Church. Bernard Häring says: "Not only false information, but especially the withholding or the arbitrary and intentional selection of relevant information, misleads. What is decisive is not the quantity of information but significant disclosure." [19] That includes facing up to unpleasant facts.

The Failure of Shared Responsibility

In the years immediately after the Second Vatican Council, diocesan and parish councils were the great hope for a more open, participatory, and declericalized approach to internal communication and decision making in the Church. In a booklet on the subject of shared responsibility published by the U.S. bishops' conference, I echoed the conventional wisdom of the mid-1970s when I wrote:

[19] Bernard Häring, *Ethics of Manipulation: Issues in Medicine, Behavior Control and Genetics* (New York: Seabury Press, 1975), 22.

Vatican II had breathed a new spirit and enunciated a new vision of the Church—as a community, a "people of God." Although in no sense did Vatican II deny, do away with, or downgrade the hierarchical structure of the Church, it made abundantly clear that hierarchical structure does not exhaust its reality. It called on all Catholics to take to heart the obvious but sometimes overlooked fact that we are all in this thing called Church together.

"'Shared responsibility' was the formula under which this fact came to be expressed", I added, and parish and diocesan councils were the institutional form it took at the local level.[20] (The unhappy fate of shared responsibility at the national level in the Church in the United States is a separate subject to be examined in the final chapter of this book.)

Diocesan and parish pastoral councils and finance councils are firmly grounded in the Code of Canon Law, but there are some significant differences in ways they are treated. Canon 511 says each diocese is to have a pastoral council, but this is followed by the important qualifier "to the extent that pastoral circumstances recommend it". The task of the diocesan pastoral council, acting "under the authority of the bishop", is "to investigate ... all those things which pertain to pastoral works, to ponder them and to propose practical conclusions about them". Canon 512 prescribes that the membership shall be priests, persons in consecrated life, and laity "of proven faith, good morals and outstanding prudence". The diocesan pastoral council enjoys "only a consultative vote", and the decision whether to make its proceedings public is up to "the bishop alone" (canon 514).

---

[20] Russell Shaw, introduction to *Shared Responsibility at Work: The Catholic Bishops' Advisory Council, 1969–1974*, ed. Michael J. Sheehan and Russell Shaw (Washington: United States Catholic Conference, 1975), 3.

As for parish pastoral councils, canon 536 says they are to be established if the local bishop "judges it opportune". Where they exist, parish councils serve in an advisory capacity to the pastor and have "consultative vote only".

Canon law is more forceful on the subject of finance councils. A diocesan finance council composed of at least three lay people is mandatory in every diocese (canon 492). This council prepares the diocesan budget (canon 493) and has some supervisory responsibility in relation to the diocesan finance officer (canon 494). At the parochial level, too, "each parish is to have a finance council" responsible for assisting the pastor in the administration of the parish (canon 537).

Despite the restrictions on what these bodies were allowed to do, much enthusiasm greeted their arrival on the scene after Vatican II. It appeared that shared responsibility was on the way to becoming an accepted fact in the Church, and most people assumed that that was a good thing. But the enthusiasm has dimmed in the last three decades. Not much is expected from these struggling vehicles of shared responsibility now. There are several reasons for that.

One reason is that time and again Church leadership just hasn't followed through. A veteran pastor—a good and conscientious man—gave me this explanation of why he had not set up a pastoral council in his parish: "If I need advice, I know where to get it—I don't need a council to tell me." Elsewhere, councils rapidly became rubber stamps for the decisions of bishops and clergy. Today, moreover, many diocesan and parish councils operate under such a heavy cloak of secrecy that few Catholics know, and even fewer care, whether they exist or what they are doing. Who the members are, when they meet and what the agenda is, what advice they give and what the bishop or pastor does about it—these matters are shrouded in deep secrecy for the vast majority of people.

Part of the problem is the sheer lack of publicity and exposure. Noting that 83 percent of Catholics in a national opinion poll said lay people should have "the right to participate in deciding how parish income should be spent", one writer pointed out that pastoral councils and finance councils already exist in almost 90 percent of American parishes. So why this "huge gap" between reality (consultative structures already exist) and perception (lay people do not have the opportunity to participate in financial decisions)?

Seeking an answer, the writer did a random search of three hundred parish Web sites. The results were revealing: 52 percent of the parishes gave the names of parish council members, but only 28 percent named the members of their finance councils; no parish Web site carried minutes of pastoral council or finance council meetings; and "not a single annual financial report for the 2004 fiscal year was found." In some cases, of course, information missing from parish Web sites may be published in parish bulletins or mailed to registered parishioners or simply posted at the back of the church; but it is likely that in many cases none of these things is done. The writer's simple conclusion: "Pastors must learn to improve communications with their parishioners." [21]

So they must.

It may not be an accident that the bright hopes for diocesan and parish councils that flourished after Vatican II have not been realized. Father John Beal writes:

> In recent years, numerous authoritative teachings and legal documents have slowly limited the scope of lay

[21] Francis Kelly Scheets, O.S.C., "Most Parishes Have Pastoral Councils, Don't They?" *Priest*, March 2006.

participation in the church's sanctifying and teaching functions, but especially in its governing function. Thus, requirements that church authorities consult before acting have
been treated as burdensome formalities to be endured before
giving effect to decisions already made, and efforts to expand
the areas in which councils involving lay people have a
deliberative vote have met with resolute resistance.[22]

That is to say: the habit of clericalist dominance, using secrecy
as its tool, has been the undoing of shared responsibility in
the Church in the United States.

Weakening Community

Secrecy, deception, stonewalling, spin, rejection of accountability, repudiation of shared responsibility and consultation—
these are deadly foes of internal communication among
members of any group. They subvert and eventually destroy
community and "horizontal" communion in the Church.
Systematically practiced by leaders at the expense of the
led, the abuse of secrecy creates an us–versus–them mentality on both sides of the relationship; for although secrecy
can have the benign result of fostering "a sense of broth-
erhood, loyalty, and equality among insiders", Sissela Bok
says, it also has the invidious result of encouraging "discrimination against outsiders".[23] Bok speaks of "the discrimination, at the heart of all secrecy, between insider and
outsider, between those set apart and all others".

---

[22] Beal, "It Shall Not Be So", 92. The passage has footnote references to
instructions from the Congregation for Bishops, Congregation for the Evangelization of Peoples, and Congregation for the Clergy.

[23] Sissela Bok, *Secrets: On the Ethics of Concealment and Revelation* (New
York: Vintage Books, 1989), xvi.

Such discrimination is one thing when it sets an individual apart as unique and protects his privacy. It is quite another thing for a group. The criteria selected for inclusion or exclusion may then lead to discriminatory action toward those excluded—on racial grounds, perhaps, or on sexual, political, or religious ones. . . .

Even where persuasive reasons for collective practices of secrecy can be stated, accountability is indispensable.[24]

In the Church, internal communication is an indispensable element of communion. The ecclesiologist William Henn, O.F.M. Cap., explains:

Jesus offered people an intimate relationship with God, the Father, Son and Holy Spirit, whose life they could share in a real way as they looked forward in hope of a future glory beyond the grave. This shared life with God constituted at the same time a new life shared with one another, what the first letter of St. John calls a "communion": "that which we have seen and heard we proclaim also to you, so that you may have fellowship [communion] with us. And our fellowship [communion] is with the Father and with his Son, Jesus Christ" (1 John 1.3). The Church is the communion of persons who are one in the Triune God.[25]

The chapter that follows makes the case for openness. There I shall begin to unpack some practical implications of this beautiful, crucially important vision of communion among the members of a Church community in communion with God.

[24] Ibid., 109–10.

[25] William Henn, O.F.M. Cap., *Church: The People of God* (London: Burns and Oates, 2004), 18–19.

Chapter Five

A CASE FOR OPENNESS

If the case for openness and accountability in human affairs generally is a strong one, the case for living by these values in the Catholic Church is even stronger. It lies in the fact that the Church is a *communio*—a unique divine-human community whose human members also are bonded to one another in and through their "membership" in Jesus Christ and the action of the Holy Spirit. In this *communio* all should be, and should act as, mature, contributing members. All should know what they need to know for that to come about.

Let me make it clear at the start that I am not setting out to demonstrate that the pastors of the Church are obliged to practice openness and accountability in every imaginable situation. Secrecy and confidentiality have their place in Church life, and sometimes a very important one. But, the special case of the seal of the confessional always excepted, the presumption in the Church's day-in, day-out life should favor openness and accountability; the burden of proof should rest with those who advocate secrecy in any particular case. The following considerations will help show why that's so.

I begin with some basic principles relating to communication, secrecy, and the news media. Next comes the heart of the argument, which concerns accountability in the

Church (in the loose sense in which it applies in that context), along with secrecy, communication, and communion.

The distinguished ethicist and moral theologian Germain Grisez discusses secrecy in the second volume of his
monumental work *The Way of the Lord Jesus*, in a chapter
titled "Equal Dignity, Communication, Interpersonal Relationships, and Restitution".[1] Equal dignity and interpersonal relationships are obviously related, and the duty to
make restitution can arise from betraying secrets. But where
do communication and secrecy fit in?

Upon reflection, however, this grouping of topics makes
good sense as a setting for considering secrecy. The fundamental questions about secrecy are, after all, whether to communicate something or not, and to whom to communicate it
and whom to exclude. Equal dignity and interpersonal relationships are key principles to use in answering these questions.

To understand secrecy's problematical side, we should begin
with the idea of communication. As usual with Grisez, his
treatment of communication is clear, realistic, succinct, and
comprehensive. "All communication should be open to community", he writes.

> Every act of communicating and receiving communication
> tends to draw the parties into an interpersonal relationship
> or to carry on and perhaps deepen an existing relationship.
> If the acts are motivated by charity, they will be open to
> genuine community and will tend to establish or build it
> up. But, if partners in communication do not act in ways
> open to genuine community, that will be because their acts
> somehow are not loving. Either the other party is consid-
> ered an enemy and genuine community is intentionally

[1] Germain Grisez, *The Way of the Lord Jesus*, vol. 2, *Living a Christian Life*
(Quincy, Ill.: Franciscan Press, 1993), 379–458.

excluded (for example, family members engaged in a quarrel seek to defend their self-interests and hurt one another), or the other party is considered an inferior person and genuine community seems impossible (for example, those caring for children, the sick, the elderly, and so on try to keep them calm and manageable rather than seeking mutual understanding as a basis for cooperation); or, again, the other party is regarded as a mere means to some specific end, and genuine community is considered irrelevant (for example, an advertiser may seek only to motivate people to buy a product or service, whether or not that really is in their interest); or, finally, the other party is regarded with indifference, and genuine community seems pointless (for example, people who wish to keep their distance encounter one another at a party, while traveling, or in other situations where they are required to converse).[2]

It is easy to see how this applies in the Church. Were not bishops who hushed up clergy sex abuse treating other members of the Church as inferiors and, at least in part, practicing cover-up in hopes of keeping them "calm and manageable"? Is not a religious congregation that sends out a deceptive fundraising letter attempting to exploit those who receive it as "mere means to [a] specific end"? Does not a pastor who refuses to answer a parishioner's polite, well-reasoned letters about liturgical abuse send the signal that he regards the letter writer "with indifference"?

Grisez also makes an argument for freedom of communication that is relevant to the question of public opinion in the Church. Although even honest communications "often express errors and seem to create problems," he says, nevertheless "they also reveal aspects of situations which require

[2] Ibid., 390–91.

attention if real progress is to be made and communion in the truth achieved."

> Consequently, those involved in every human association should begin with a presumption favoring freedom of speech and other modes of communicating. . . . Usually, it is better that necessary limits on communication be self-imposed by those involved . . . rather than established and enforced by authority. Therefore, people should support a strong, though rebuttable, presumption against inhibiting communication, not only in political society but in the family, the Church, and, indeed, in every community and relationship.[3]

This does not mean people always must communicate everything they have no reason to keep secret. But it does mean that if members of an organization or group desire information that there is no morally compelling reason to withhold, the people in charge violate their rights as members by keeping the information secret. This principle plainly applies to things like the Church's approach to media relations or a bishop's policy for his diocesan newspaper.

Communication and Secrecy

Grisez begins his discussion of secrecy with a clarification that might usefully be kept in mind not just in reading his treatment but in discussions of this question generally: "*Secret* does not refer here to everything any individual or society wishes to hide, but only to something that someone or some

---

[3] Ibid., 397–98. Grisez adds that the strong presumption in favor of freedom of expression truly is "rebuttable"; it should not be used to justify violations of morally justified privacy and secrecy or to override prohibitions on immoral and socially harmful activities, e.g., producing and distributing pornography.

group has some *morally acceptable reason* for hiding." [4] It would save much time and energy if secrecy in the Church lacking any morally acceptable reason could be summarily dismissed with a simple "That's wrong." Then we could move on to argue about something difficult and obscure that really needs to be argued about.

Communication is for community; openness and generosity in communicating are therefore generally good. But the goodness of secrecy, which takes for granted "outsiders" to whom the secret is not communicated, is "not so clear". Plainly, however, there are situations of intimacy where secrecy is important—intimate communication between spouses, for example; secrecy in these cases enables the parties to reveal themselves to one another "more fully than they could or rightly would to others" and contributes to building community between them. Finally, Grisez points to other reasons why secrecy can be necessary: to allow people to do good deeds without looking for praise; to protect a group's plans and strategies, preliminary drafts, and the like from others who might make bad use of them; to protect property from being unjustly taken. In view of considerations like these, he writes, "individuals sometimes rightly keep secret what they share in any particular community, and communities sometimes rightly keep secret what they share with one another." [5]

Still, this hardly amounts to a blank check for secrecy. The responsibility for keeping and respecting secrets is limited, and "under certain conditions a person should divulge or seek access to secrets." Furthermore, "even when some persons or groups continue to have a good and morally

[4] Ibid., 415.
[5] Ibid.

acceptable reason for wishing to conceal something, others sometimes can have a good and morally binding reason to investigate it." Grisez' examples include citizens who believe their government is acting illegally and wrongly in secretly preparing to go to war; public authorities who need to learn the secrets of innocent people so as to tell the innocent from the guilty; physicians and public health workers who need to disclose the identities of persons with a deadly but usually not contagious disease in order to prevent it from spreading.[6] The author recommends using the Golden Rule of fairness—treat others as you would have them treat you—in deciding whether to keep secrets or not keep them.

And the Church? Grisez earlier makes the point that the Church is a divine-human communion uniting human persons with God in Christ and thus bonding them to one another. As a uniquely intimate communion, the Church is unlike any political society; it more nearly resembles a family. But it would be a mistake simply to leave it at that. Grisez explains why:

> Unfortunately, pervasive and longstanding clericalism, by reducing the laity to passivity and treating as normative forms of spirituality proper to priests and religious, has given Catholics a misleading experience of the Church. All too often the faithful feel themselves to be, not brothers and sisters joined in in intimate communion and full cooperators in carrying out the Church's mission, but citizens in a rather weak monarchic or aristocratic political society, whose government lacks necessary checks and balances, and whose inefficient clerical and lay bureaucracy often is impervious to advice and criticism.[7]

[6] Ibid., 416–17.
[7] Ibid., 161.

The abuse of secrecy makes the situation worse. That the Church is a unique communion of faith and love does not justify those in authority in ignoring "the conditions necessary for the just use of authority in any human community", including consulting the opinions of members.[8] Moreover, the family analogy is not helpful where secrecy in the Church is the issue. Parents have many good reasons for keeping many things from children until they are mature: they would not understand; it would just upset them to know; they might tell outsiders who have no business knowing. But considerations like these do not apply to adult members of the Church, who need information in order to cooperate with the Church's leaders and with one another in a mature, responsible way.

Of Individuals and Groups

Sissela Bok is of particular interest for her two book-length studies—of lying and of secrecy—that take contemporary American circumstances and attitudes specifically into account.[9] As a secular ethicist, Bok takes an approach radically different from that of Germain Grisez and others in the Catholic tradition. The orientation is utilitarian/consequentialist: while there are some things from which every decent person spontaneously recoils, nothing can be absolutely excluded in advance; actions that are generally wrong could, at least in theory, sometimes be right, depending on circumstances and the calculus of good and bad results.

[8] Ibid., 165.
[9] Sissela Bok, *Lying: Moral Choice in Public and Private Life* (first published in 1978; second paperback edition, New York: Vintage Books, 1999); *Secrets: On the Ethics of Concealment and Revelation* (first published in 1983; paperback edition, New York: Vintage Books, 1989).

Those who subscribe to an ethic of moral absolutes, which recognizes that some things may never be directly willed regardless of circumstances or results, will naturally find Bok's basic approach unacceptable, and this in turn will render her conclusions more or less suspect in their eyes. Still, the testimony of a consequentialist like Bok is of interest in thinking about something like secrecy, where decisions often require prudential determinations. If someone open to the possibility that what is usually wrong may sometimes be right nevertheless judges a particular instance of secrecy to be an abuse, then even the consequentialist calculus apparently tips against secrecy in this case.

Bok takes a benign view of secrecy when the intent is to protect individual privacy. She concedes, however, that secrecy is dangerous, especially as a tool in the hands of persons who have power over others.

> For all individuals, secrecy carries some risk of corruption and of irrationality; if they dispose of greater than ordinary power over others, and if this power is exercised in secret, with no accountability to those whom it affects, the invitation to abuse is great.... Long-term group practices of secrecy ... are especially likely to breed corruption. Every aspect of the shared predicament influences the secret practice cumulatively over time: in particular the impediments to reasoning and to choice, and the limitations on sympathy and on regard for human beings. The tendency to view the world in terms of insiders and outsiders can then build up a momentum that it would lack if it were short-lived and immediately accountable.[10]

The presumption in favor of secrecy (where the privacy of individuals is concerned) becomes a presumption against

[10] Bok, *Secrets*, 106, 110.

secrecy when it is the secrecy of groups. The burden of proof rests with those who would deny the secrecy claims of individuals who seek to protect their personal privacy; but in the case of secrecy exercised by a group with power over others, the burden of justifying secrecy rests with the group, as does the duty to show what kinds of safeguards it means to put in place to prevent abuses from occurring.[11]

This suggests that a group's deliberations about adopting a policy of secrecy should be conducted publicly as a way of forestalling abuse, with the pros and cons of secrecy set out for examination by those who will be affected by the decision.[12] One might point out that in imposing secrecy on portions of their general meetings that deal with matters directly affecting the interests of the other members of the Church, the bishops of the United States have not done anything of the sort. Not only are the reasons for keeping individual matters secret not revealed (as one might expect), but, more to the point, the general criteria that justify its practice of secrecy have not been stated by the bishops' national conference.

The practice of secrecy by individuals and groups is a standing temptation for them to engage in deception and other, even worse, abuses. Bok observes, "Even where persuasive reasons for collective practices of secrecy can be stated, accountability is indispensable. . . . No such safeguards have accompanied the many secret police systems that have plagued humanity." [13]

[11] Ibid., 110.

[12] See ibid., 114. Bok concedes that this is not realistically possible in some circumstances, e.g., under repressive regimes, and may be greeted with public indifference even where it is done. That, of course, is not an argument for not doing it.

[13] Ibid., 110–11.

The Role of a Free Press

A large part of secrecy, openness, and accountability by the
Church involves her relationship with the news media. This
relationship has always been more or less adversarial, and it
remains so today. Both sides share responsibility for that unsatisfactory state of affairs.

As we also saw earlier, the neo-Thomist Catholic phi-
losopher Jacques Maritain contended that the hostility toward
freedom of the press and freedom of expression voiced in
the nineteenth century by Church leaders like popes Gregory XVI and Pius IX arose from their opposition to treating these values as if they were "ends in themselves and
unlimited rights". Maritain wrote: "These freedoms are good
and answer to radical needs in human nature [but] they have
to be regulated, as does everything that is not of the order
of Deity itself." [14]

Maritain may have been straining to give a positive inter-
pretation to the condemnations of press freedom by churchmen of the past. But even if he were correct, the fact
remains that the record of the Catholic Church in the last
two centuries was undistinguished, to say the least, on
this matter of recognizing the societal importance of free
news media and upholding their rights. To be sure, the
press is very far from perfect, and the Church often has
suffered unjustly from journalists' ignorance and bias; I
have often written about these problems myself.[15] With
all their faults, though, free news media are indispensable

[14] Jacques Maritain, *Integral Humanism: Temporal and Spiritual Problems of a New Christendom* (New York: Charles Scribner's Sons, 1968), 182.

[15] See, for instance, Russell Shaw, "The Church and the Media: Who's to Blame?" in *Anti-Catholicism in American Culture*, ed. Robert P. Lockwood (Huntington, Ind.: Our Sunday Visitor Publishing Division, 2000), 105–31.

to a democratic society, and the Church on the whole has taken surprisingly little notice of that extremely important fact.

Pope John XXIII's affirmation in *Pacem in Terris* of the human right to "freedom of speech and publication" (to be exercised "within the limits of the moral order and the common good") was a breakthrough in its day.[16] More typical was the guarded approach taken less than eight months later by the Second Vatican Council's Decree on the Means of Social Communication, *Inter Mirifica*. It coupled the acknowledgment that, "properly used", the media can be "of considerable benefit to mankind" with the cautious observation that "man can use them in ways that are contrary to the Creator's design and damaging to himself."[17] Undoubtedly that is so, someone might reply—but could not a general council of the Catholic Church find anything more helpful and illuminating to say?

It is disconcerting to find a Catholic writer even today apparently unable simply to say that press freedom is on the whole a very good thing. While complaining that decisions of the European Union (EU) are "taken without democratic process and are kept out of the public eye" and arguing the case for "more openness" in EU affairs, this writer makes the remarkable statement that in the final analysis a free press is not really necessary. After all, "one can imagine a country in which the government and local administrators provide the necessary information through public announcers."[18]

---

[16] Pope John XIII, *Pacem in Terris* (Peace on Earth) (April 11, 1963), no. 12.

[17] Vatican Council II, Decree on the Means of Social Communication, *Inter Mirifica* (December 4, 1963), no. 2.

[18] Leo Elders, "Freedom of the Press vs. the Right to Privacy", *Fellowship of Catholic Scholars Quarterly*, Spring 2006.

Perhaps this is meant only as a hypothetical aside, without intending endorsement of the idea; but even as a hypothetical aside, it is unacceptable. There is no need to *imagine* a country like that; the experiment has been tried as a matter of actual, historical fact—in Hitler's Germany, Stalin's Soviet Union, Mao's China, and other totalitarian states. It seems not to have worked very well. Mental gymnastics like this contrast painfully with the straightforward words of an Arab journalist who lost his job as columnist with a Saudi Arabian newspaper for criticizing oppressive Islamic regimes: "A free press, a truly free press, is a moral imperative in society. Subvert it, and you subvert the public's sacrosanct right to know and a newspaper's traditional role to expose." [19]

Sissela Bok nevertheless dismisses arguments for the public's right to know as "patently inadequate". [20] This appears to be a quibble arising from the admittedly limited human ability to know the facts about anything. But claims for the right to know are not based on the assumption that people can know everything; they are based on the modest view—in turn based on fairness—that most of the time people with relevant information have an obligation to share it with others who need it to protect their legitimate interests. Bok is on firmer ground a few pages later, saying the public's right to know is a right of "access to information"; the public, she explains, has "a legitimate interest in all information about matters that might affect its welfare". [21] That is true in the Church as well as in civil society.

[19] Fawaz Turki, "How to Lose Your Job at a Saudi Newspaper", *Washington Post*, April 14, 2006.

[20] Bok, *Secrets*, 254.

[21] Ibid., 258.

It is true that the complexity of some issues in the public, governmental sphere limits the immediate *right* to information to those with the specialized expertise to understand the information, evaluate it, and respond to it in the public interest. But that simply underlines the fact that, absent compelling reasons for secrecy, such information *should* be released to those who are able to handle it.

As for the Church, the issues that arise there are seldom so complex that ordinary people are incapable of understanding them. If explanations are needed—for example, about various aspects of detailed financial reports—then provide the explanations. Telling people that a parish priest has been removed because he sexually misbehaved with a minor would not have been giving them information they could not handle; it would simply have made it impossible to send the man to another parish in a few months, to be placed in charge of the altar boys by an unsuspecting pastor.

The Church and the Press

The importance of a free press in a democratic society points to certain conclusions about the stance to the news media that the Church should take.

Ethics in Communications, the document published in 2000 by the Pontifical Council for Social Communications to mark a "jubilee of journalists" during the third millennium jubilee proclaimed by Pope John Paul II, underscored one obvious conclusion: Church officials must learn how to get along with the press. "The Church would be well served if more of those who hold offices and perform functions in her name received communication training. This is true not only of seminarians, persons in formation in religious communities, and young lay Catholics, but Church personnel generally." [22]

One reason bishops needlessly resort to closed-door meetings and other secretive practices is that many of them just do not like journalists, do not trust them, and do not feel comfortable having them around. It is not hard to sympathize with bishops who feel like that. Not all journalists are charming people, and not all bishops are natural media stars. Persons of a reserved temperament may well find giving interviews and holding news conferences a painful chore. But it is possible to learn how to do these things, and one's comfort level rises measurably with practice. [23] Accepting the presence of reporters and dealing with them in a professional manner are necessary elements in the job descriptions of leaders of today's large public institutions, including leaders of the Catholic Church. Executive sessions behind closed doors are not the answer to uneasiness with the media; training and practice are.

Ethics in Communications also speaks of internal communication in the Church in a passage that recalls earlier statements: "A two-way flow of information and views between pastors and faithful, freedom of expression sensitive to the well being of the community and to the role of the Magisterium ... and responsible public opinion all are important expressions of 'the fundamental right of dialogue and information within the Church'" (reference to the pastoral

---

[22] Pontifical Council for Social Communications, *Ethics in Communications* (June 4, 2000), no. 26.

[23] A notable example of this in my experience was Joseph Cardinal Bernardin. When I worked with him in the early 1970s at the U.S. bishops' conference, he genuinely dreaded encounters with journalists. But he taught himself to handle the media with great skill and by the end of his life was a master of the art.

instructions *Aetatis Novae*, no. 10, and *Communio et Progressio*, no. 20).

Finally, *Ethics in Communications* makes a plea for openness in Church communication.

> Like other communities and institutions, the Church sometimes needs—in fact, is sometimes obliged—to practice secrecy and confidentiality. But this should not be for the sake of manipulation and control. Within the communion of faith, "holders of office, who are invested with a sacred power, are, in fact, dedicated to promoting the interests of their brethren, so that all who belong to the People of God, and are consequently endowed with true Christian dignity, may through their free and well-ordered efforts toward a common good, attain to salvation" (*Lumen Gentium*, 18). Right practice in communication is one of the ways of realizing this vision. (no. 26)

Accountability in the Church

Lumen Gentium's statement that those who hold sacred power in the Church are "dedicated to promoting the interests of their brethren" calls attention to the question of accountability. Are bishops and other holders of ecclesiastical office such as religious superiors, who exercise authority in their own names or the names of others, accountable to those whom they serve concerning how good a job they do in promoting the interests of the latter? It is impossible to find a clear, direct statement by an authoritative source saying they are. That in itself suggests the existence of some sort of problem. Accountability in its strict sense does not apply in the Church; but accountability in a looser, general sense most certainly does apply, and the not uncommon failure to acknowledge that is dismaying in itself.

It is universally taken for granted in democratic societies today that leaders are accountable to those whom they lead. Of course that does not mean the principle of accountability is universally observed—leaders often fail in this matter due to ignorance, arrogance, and corruption. But at least the failures are condemned when they become publicly known, and the principle still stands. Public officials who fail in accountability usually do not remain in elective office very long. In recent times, abuses of authority in a variety of institutions, from universities to multinational corporations, have spurred efforts on behalf of greater accountability.

Considered in this context, Yale political scientist Bruce Russett remarks, the governing structures of the Church "stand out as an anomaly": only rudimentary structures of ecclesiastical accountability have been created up to now; and as the scandal of clerical sex abuse has made painfully evident, up to now they have not worked very well.[24]

Church authorities usually respond to criticism of this sort by saying that the Church is not a political society and, in particular, not a democracy. That observation unquestionably is true. This is the reason why accountability in the strict sense does not apply in the Church: the faithful are not superior to the pastors and do not have a right to discharge them if the pastors are found wanting in the performance of their duties. But the Church does have structures and processes of governance, and, with reason, Catholics often perceive these in a markedly political—and more-or-less unfavorable—light: they are viewed as the

[24] Bruce Russett, "Monarchy, Democracy, or 'Decent Consultation Hierarchy?'" in *Governance, Accountability, and the Future of the Catholic Church*, ed. Francis Oakley and Bruce Russett (New York: Continuum, 2004), 197–99.

elements of a hierarchical polity in which accountability appropriate to the community of faith is lacking—or, as Germain Grisez says, "a rather weak monarchic or aristocratic political society, whose government lacks necessary checks and balances, and whose inefficient clerical and lay bureaucracy often is impervious to advice and criticism." [25]

A paper by intelligent and thoughtful prelate, Archbishop Donald W. Wuerl of Washington, deserves close attention for what it says, and what it does not say, about accountability. Archbishop Wuerl, who was bishop of Pittsburgh at the time the paper was written and delivered, makes the familiar point that the Church is not a democracy; moreover, "because of sacred orders, the priest stands in the midst of the church as its leader, its head." [26] At the same time, he acknowledges a need for "much greater participation" by the laity in consultative roles in which they are heard and taken seriously by the people in charge. [27]

And accountability? Archbishop Wuerl says the key concept in the Church is the "obedience of faith"—fidelity to the revelation entrusted to the Church by God. [28] This of course is very different from strict accountability of pastors to people. It is "a temptation", he remarks, "to make the church into an American democratic organization as if we, the members, had supreme authority over the body. We do not vote or take a headcount to determine what we should believe or how the church should be structured. But we

---

[25] Grisez, *Living a Christian Life*, 161.
[26] Most Reverend Donald W. Wuerl, "Reflections on Governance and Accountability in the Church", in Oakley and Russett, *Governance*, 16.
[27] Ibid., 23–24.
[28] Ibid., 14.

are called to see that the whole church is faithful to its identity and mission."[29]

No doubt some Catholics today are tempted to suppose that a form of naïve democratization would be a legitimate and desirable option for the Church. Pope Benedict XVI therefore rightly warns against applying models drawn from secular politics to the task of interpreting what the Second Vatican Council meant in calling the community of faith "the People of God".[30] Others, though, simply wish to make the point that the Church, which has adapted the forms of various other systems of governance to her own circumstances and needs in other times and places, could also do the same with some democratic forms today without compromising her essential structure.

As for the need to ensure that, in Archbishop Wuerl's words, "the whole church is faithful to its identity and mission", one indispensable way of doing that today is precisely by expanding the practice of accountability, understood as extending both upward (from people to their local pastors, from pastors to their bishops, and from bishops to the pope) but also downward: the accountability of the leaders to the rank-and-file People of God.

As Archbishop Wuerl points out, the concept of "higher authority" is central to accountability in the Church;[31] but so is the realization that higher authority has real obligations to those it is appointed to serve and that it is answerable to people for how well it lives up to its responsibilities.

[29] Ibid., 17.

[30] See, for example, Joseph Cardinal Ratzinger, "The Ecclesiology of the Constitution *Lumen Gentium*", in *Pilgrim Fellowship of Faith: The Church as Communion*, ed. Stephan Otto Horn and Vinzenz Pfnur (San Francisco: Ignatius Press, 2005), 127.

[31] Wuerl, "Reflections", 21.

This is accountability in the loose sense that it rightly has in the Church. And, as Archbishop Wuerl points out, "openness" is the key. "Whatever our responsibility, we must exercise it with an openness that takes the form of sharing information, reporting on the discharge of our duties, and accepting critique of our actions. . . . [I]f we exercise public ecclesial service . . . then we should be accountable before the whole church for how well we do."[32]

Secrecy is the bane of accountability. A veteran editor, explaining why newspapers publish government secrets, says: "Secrecy and security are not the same. . . . Accountability is only possible when citizens . . . know what is going on. None of us has ever been held accountable for an act no one knew we committed."[33] One need not suppose that the media never err in this matter or that those who leak information always deserve applause,[34] to agree that this rationale is correct. Change "security" to "orthodoxy" and "citizens" to "Catholics", however, and it also applies to the Church.

Archbishop Wuerl sees accountability in the Church as being in generally good shape: "The structures already exist", he says. In other words: the structures of consultation and

[32] Ibid., 18.

[33] Robert G. Kaiser, "Public Secrets", *Washington Post*, June 11, 2006.

[34] An example in the Church of a case in which those who leaked confidential information did *not* deserve applause was the leaking of the so-called majority report of the papal "birth control commission" before the publication of Pope Paul VI's 1968 encyclical on contraception, *Humanae Vitae*. The process leading up to the encyclical, including the secrecy—at once excessive and ineffectual—undoubtedly left much to be desired, and the non-response to this leak was a serious tactical mistake. But none of that excuses those responsible for leaking the report, who violated a trust they had voluntarily accepted in a transparent attempt to place external pressure on the pope.

accountability adopted after Vatican Council II—presbyteral councils, finance councils, and pastoral councils on the diocesan level and parish levels—exist and are working. Literally, that is true; it appears that these bodies generally are in place in the United States. But it would be wrong to think that all of them are functioning well. As we saw in the last chapter, the aura of hope surrounding them in the years after Vatican II has long since disappeared; today they strike many people as window dressing at most.

The clergy sex abuse scandal lends support to that view. A veteran observer of the Church remarks, "One of the most salient aspects of the sexual abuse crisis is the remarkable silence of lay boards and church lay councils throughout the nation." [35] Building openness and trust in the Church in the United States will require breathing life back into these moribund bodies.

Taking a New Look at Accountability

To do that, we have to take a fresh look at accountability in the Church. Here are a few thoughts on that.

The pastors of the Church are accountable in a strict sense to God. But this accountability has a specific content— preaching the gospel and serving the People of God, as Jesus commanded in telling Peter: "Feed my sheep" (Jn 21:17).

What does this "feeding" consist in? Doing it and doing it well requires meeting people's spiritual needs (sound doctrine, the availability of the sacraments, the Church's life of worship and prayer) and also keeping people informed about the affairs of the Church so that they can carry out *their* part

[35] Francis J. Butler, "Financial Accountability: Reflections on Giving and Church Leadership", in Oakley and Russett, *Governance*, 158.

in her mission, making *their* special contribution to spreading the good news. The serious obligation that pastors have to do these things is the basis of accountability in its loose sense.

It does not empower the people to judge and depose pastors whom they find wanting. But it does allow them to make evaluations and recommendations—even to make corrections where they are in order. The pastors of the Church need this input and should facilitate it by readily supplying information and establishing structures and processes for it to take place. It is an important help to them in correcting their mistakes and oversights, and also in gauging what needs correcting in the knowledge and attitudes of the faithful. Here is why public opinion in the Church is so important; and it requires an open, ongoing, two-way flow of information, not top-down, one-way communication in combination with official secrecy about matters the pastors find it convenient to keep to themselves.

Beyond that, there are two areas in the life of the Catholic community where accountability of this sort is particularly relevant: money and the spiritual life.

It is axiomatic in a society committed to the fundamental equality in dignity and rights of its members that those who solicit money for good causes make an implicit—and sometimes explicit—promise to the donors to use their gifts for the purposes indicated and to give a public accounting showing this was done. This rule holds in the Church, but it frequently is violated there. Parishioners are asked to contribute to causes whose purposes are only sketchily explained, and seldom do they get an accounting of how the money was spent. In the absence of extenuating circumstances, that is inexcusable.

Furthermore, even though the Church's faithful do not choose their leaders, as members of a democratic society

do theirs, they do freely choose to accept and cooperate
with the spiritual leaders of parishes and dioceses who are
given to them. In doing so, they entrust themselves to these
leaders to receive formation in the faith and participate in
the sacraments—indeed, they entrust themselves in regard
to their spiritual well-being as a whole. This free acceptance and entrustment give rise to an obligation on the pastors' part to do what the faithful rightly expect of them. As
Archbishop Wuerl says: "[I]f we exercise public ecclesial service ... then we should be accountable before the whole
church for how well we do."

It is often said that people in positions of authority in
the Church are accountable to those who appointed them
to office but *not* to those they were appointed to serve. But
that confuses legitimacy with accountability. In general, the
legitimacy of holders of Church offices comes from the fact
that they have been legitimately appointed or at least confirmed by ecclesiastical superiors, not from the vote or
approval of those they rule.[36] But it would be wildly wide
of the mark to suppose that their legitimacy as officeholders somehow cancels their obligation and answerability to
the people they are appointed to serve.

A view of accountability that limits it to the model
of upward accountability only (laity to priests, priests to

[36] There are exceptions: e.g., a religious congregation in which the superior is chosen by the members or some designated body representing them.
It should also be kept in mind that in the early centuries of the Church,
acceptance by the people was commonly considered to be a necessary part
of the process by which a man became a bishop. See Yves Congar, O.P.,
Lay People in the Church, revised edition (London: Geoffrey Chapman, 1985),
244ff. Congar writes, for example: "The elements guaranteeing valid episcopal institution are enumerated by Cyprian thus: judgement of God, good
recommendation by the clergy, suffrage of the people, consent of other
bishops."

bishops, bishops to the pope) takes for granted an ecclesiology according to which authority flows only downward.
This is sometimes called a "pyramidal view" of the Church.
In his well-known book *Models of the Church*, Avery Cardinal Dulles, S.J., speaks of "the pyramidal pattern in which
all power is conceived as descending from the pope through
the bishops and priests, while at the base the faithful people play a passive role and seem to have a lower position in
the Church".[37] Inasmuch as the Church is hierarchical and
institutional, this view is at least partly correct; but to take
it as the *sole* and *comprehensive* legitimate way of thinking of
the Church is a mistake that breeds more mistakes.

Beginning at least with Pope Pius XII's 1943 encyclical
Mystici Corporis Christi (On the Mystical Body of Christ),
the Magisterium of the Church in modern times has sought
a formula to express an earlier view according to which
the Church, rather than being only a top-down power pyr-
amid, is a hierarchically structured community of persons
fundamentally equal in their dignity and rights as community members. This view of the Church does not destroy
the authority of the clerical hierarchy, but it situates authority in a context in which it is understood as a service
rendered to some by others, all of them engaged in living
out their particular vocations. It reaches a high point in
Lumen Gentium, Vatican II's Dogmatic Constitution on the
Church.

> There is, therefore, one chosen People of God: "one Lord,
> one faith, one baptism" (Eph. 4.5); there is a common dig-
> nity of members deriving from their rebirth in Christ, a
> common grace as sons, a common vocation to perfection,

[37] Avery Dulles, S.J., *Models of the Church* (Garden City, N.Y.: Doubleday
Image Books, 1978), 44.

one salvation, one hope and undivided charity. In Christ
and in the Church there is, then, no inequality arising from
race or nationality, social condition or sex, for "there is neither Jew nor Greek; there is neither slave nor freeman; there
is neither male nor female. For you are all 'one' in Christ
Jesus" (Gal. 3.28 Greek; cf. Col. 3.11).[38]

The dogmatic constitution goes on to note the diversity
of offices and charisms in the Church and the indispensable reality of hierarchy. Then it says: "The distinction which
the Lord has made between the sacred ministers and the
rest of the People of God involves union.... [A]mid
variety all will bear witness to the wonderful unity in the
Body of Christ: this very diversity of graces, of ministries
and of works gathers the sons of God into one, for 'all
these things are the work of the one and the same Spirit'
(1 Cor. 12.11)."[39]

This vision of the Church today is commonly called "the
ecclesiology of communion". Vertical communion—the
Church's intimate union with the triune God—comes first;
but ecclesial communion also has an inseparable horizontal dimension—the communion of the Church's members
with one another, in and through Christ and his Spirit.
William Henn says: "Communion with the risen Lord estab-
lishes also a communion between the believers themselves.... If the Church is people of God, body of Christ
and temple of the Holy Spirit, then its life should reflect
the communion and mission which are contained in that
wonderful saying of St. John: 'God is love, and he who

---

[38] Vatican Council II, Dogmatic Constitution on the Church, *Lumen Gentium* (November 21, 1964), no. 32.
[39] Ibid.

abides in love abides in God, and God abides in him'
(1 John 4.16)." [40]

The Implications of Communion

Communion exists not only among the structural elements
of the Church, such as particular churches (the "Oriental
Churches", the "Western Church", etc.) and local churches
(dioceses, eparchies), but also among the individual members. A passage from *Lumen Gentium* suggests the complex
reality.

> In virtue of this catholicity each part contributes its own
> gifts to other parts and to the whole Church, so that the
> whole and each of the parts are strengthened by the com-
> mon sharing of all things and by the common effort to
> attain to fullness in unity. Hence it is that the People of
> God is not only an assembly of various peoples, but in itself
> is made up of different ranks. This diversity among its mem-
> bers is either by reason of their duties—some exercise the
> sacred ministry for the good of their brethren—or it is due
> to their condition and manner of life—many enter the reli-
> gious state and, intending to sanctity by the narrower way,
> stimulate their brethren by their example. Holding a right-
> ful place in the communion of the Church there are also
> particular Churches that retain their own traditions, with-
> out prejudice to the Chair of Peter. . . . Finally, between all
> the various parts of the Church there is a bond of close
> communion whereby spiritual riches, apostolic workers and
> temporal resources are shared. For the members of the Peo-
> ple of God are called upon to share their goods, and the
> words of the apostle apply also to each of the Churches,

[40] William Henn, O.F.M. Cap., *Church: The People of God* (London: Burns
and Oates, 2004), 43–44.

"according to the gift that each has received, administer it
to one another as good stewards of the manifold grace of
God" (Pet. 4.10).[41]

As Pope Benedict points out, the ecclesiology of Vatican II
is distorted by reducing communion either to "the relationship between the local Church and the Church as a
whole" or to "egalitarianism" among her members: the primacy of the vertical dimension of communion—the relationship with God—must always be respected. After that,
the complexity of communion's horizontal dimension—
the relationship of local church to universal church, and of
individual member to individual member—must be kept
clearly in view.[42]

As a product of the presence and activity of the Spirit,
communion cannot be equated with ordinary human communication, and certainly not with simple fellowship and
kindly feelings, however desirable these may be; yet communion and communication are not really separable either.
To suppose otherwise would be still another form of
reductionism—communion as a disincarnate, purely "spiritual" reality. No one is more bitingly critical than Pope
Benedict of those whose ecclesiology is an affair of power
and "privileges"; yet even he is careful to point out: "That
does not mean that the argument about the right ordering
of things ... should not also be carried on in the Church." [43]
And elsewhere he stresses "the necessity of a visible Church
and of visible, concrete (one might say, 'institutional')
unity".[44]

---

[41] *Lumen Gentium*, no. 13.

[42] Ratzinger, "Ecclesiology of the Constitution *Lumen Gentium*", 132.

[43] Ibid., 133.

[44] Ratzinger, "Communion: Eucharist—Fellowship—Mission", in ibid., 83.

Dietrich Bonhoeffer, the Lutheran pastor and theologian executed by the Nazis near the end of World War II, makes similar points in rejecting the suggestion that human beings do not owe truthfulness to other human beings but only to God.

> God is not a general principle, but the living God who has set me in a living life and who demands service of me within this living life. If one speaks of God one must not simply disregard the actual given world in which one lives; for if one does that one is not speaking of the God who entered into the world in Jesus Christ, but rather of some metaphysical idol.... The truthfulness which we owe to God must assume a concrete form in the world. Our speech must be truthful, not in principle but concretely. A truthfulness which is not concrete is not truthful before God.[45]

Nor are we entitled to make a metaphysical idol of ecclesial communion by divorcing it from issues of interpersonal communication among members of the Church. The concrete realization of communion in the historical circumstances of real-world Christianity requires open, ongoing communication.

That is clear from a passage in Saint Paul's first letter to the Corinthians in which he rebukes the Christians of Corinth for abuses in celebrating the Eucharist. The Eucharist is the bond of communion par excellence among members of the Church, but the bad behavior of the Corinthians has turned it into a setting for the acting out of conflicts. Among other problems, Paul remarks, there are "divisions among you" when the Corinthian Christians "assemble as a church"; and in these circumstances of

---

[45] Dietrich Bonhoeffer, *Ethics* (New York: Macmillan, 1965), 364.

fractured relationship, "when you come together it is not for the better but for the worse." Aberrations like this are no small matter, he points out, since "whoever ... eats the bread or drinks the cup of the Lord in an unworthy manner will be guilty of profaning the body and blood of the Lord" (see 1 Cor 11:17–29).

In other words: the Eucharist does not work by magic; grace really does build on nature, and good human dispositions and actions—including honest communication—are required if the Eucharist is to forge bonds of communion among fractious Christians.

This same concern with the quality of communication and its relationship to communion can also be seen in Paul's discussion of the gift of tongues in chapter 14 of 1 Corinthians. Prophecy—testimony to Christian truth—is the more important gift, he says. "For one who speaks in a tongue speaks not to men but to God; for no one understands him, but he utters mysteries in the Spirit. On the other hand, he who prophesies speaks to men for their upbuilding and encouragement and consolation. He who speaks in a tongue edifies himself, but he who prophesies edifies the church" (1 Cor 14:2–4). As an instrument of evangelization, too, the interpersonal communication involved in prophecy is far superior to tongues. "If ... the whole church assembles and all speak in tongues, and outsiders or unbelievers enter, will they not say that you are mad? But if all prophesy, and an unbeliever or outsider enters, he is convicted by all, he is called to account by all, the secrets of his heart are disclosed; and so, falling on his face, he will worship God and declare that God is really among you" (1 Cor 14:23–25).

But what do these Pauline teachings have to do with secrecy and openness in the Church? Just this: communication is essential to healthy ecclesial community and so to the realization of communion. The failure to communicate, even if it is accompanied by showy displays, falls sadly short.

When that happens, the familiar problem of clericalism is reinforced. Yves Congar says: "Pastorally, clericalism results in this, that lay people, kept in subjection and passivity in the Church, are not formed in their own Christian responsibilities, which it is their business to discharge in the world and in the course of history." [46] The ecclesiology of communion, with its implied criticism of abusive secrecy for the sake of clericalist manipulation and control, is a repudiation of all that.

These reflections do not show—in fact, they are not meant to show—the existence of an exceptionless, ironclad obligation to refrain from secrecy in Church affairs. But they do show that the presumption ought to be in favor of openness, with the burden of proof resting (the seal of the confessional excepted) on those who wish to argue for secrecy in particular cases "that involve the good name of individuals, or that touch upon the rights of people whether singly or collectively". [47]

Prudence is the rule here. But the question with which prudence must wrestle is not how to keep the Church secretive and closed, but how to make her as open as possible. It is wrong to cultivate secrecy for the sake of clericalist paternalism, the convenience of the powerful, the concealment of the faults of persons that are a threat to others, the manipulation of the lay faithful, or some combination of some or all of these motives. Communion within the community of faith deserves much better than that.

---

[46] Congar, *Lay People in the Church*, 53.

[47] Pontifical Commission for Social Communications, Pastoral Instruction on the Means of Social Communication, *Communio et Progressio* (May 23, 1971), no. 121.

Chapter Six

THE CHURCH WITH NOTHING TO HIDE

I was trying to explain to someone why it is unfair to come down too hard on today's Catholic bishops over the sex abuse scandal. Most cases of abuse that we know of, I pointed out, happened twenty, thirty, forty, or even more years ago; with few exceptions, bishops responsible for covering up crimes back then have left the scene by retirement or death; and even the most seriously erring bishops of that generation apparently believed they were doing the right thing and acting for the good of the Church. That does not excuse what happened, but it does put it in a somewhat different light, I said.

"Maybe so," my companion replied, "but it isn't going to score many points with her."

He meant a good friend of his, a Catholic woman who seldom went to church anymore, on the grounds that the sex abuse scandal and the hypocrisy of the Church's leaders had soured her on practicing her religion. She was adamant in her views, it seemed, and nothing could budge her. One could only hope that prayer, good example, and time would some day bring her back to the faith.

Perhaps she is an extreme case. On the whole, polls tell us, the response of American Catholics to the scandal has been surprisingly restrained. According to the Center for

Applied Research in the Apostolate, the rate of Sunday Mass attendance in the United States was about one Catholic in three shortly before the uproar began in early 2002 and was still one in three by the fall of 2005. (Of course, that is half the rate of forty years earlier, but at least the scandal apparently has not made this particular problem any worse.)

Catholic households similarly reported contributing financially to their parishes both before and after the scandal (74 percent, September–October 2005); but the percentage giving to diocesan appeals fell from a prescandal 38 percent to a postscandal 29 percent. There is a possible link here to the fact that only one-third of Catholics rated the bishops' handling of sex abuse positively; and by the fall of 2005 fully 74 percent said the scandal had damaged the credibility of Church leaders when they speak on social and political issues (even two-thirds of the Catholics who attend Mass weekly felt that way).[1]

If the public reaction of Catholics to the scandal has on the whole been restrained, however, a starkly different picture sometimes emerges in conversation. Even *good* Catholics—regular Mass-goers who give generously to the Church and seldom indulge in criticism—may express powerful negative feelings when they open up in private. A layman who in everyday life is a successful professional and also runs the RCIA program in his parish with great dedication and notable success summed it up to me like this:

> I live and work in a largely non-Catholic, even anti-Catholic, environment. In this setting I consider it my

[1] See Mark M. Gray and Paul M. Perl, *Catholic Reactions to the News of Sexual Abuse Cases Involving Catholic Clergy* (Washington, D.C.: Center for Applied Research in the Apostolate, 2006).

job to be an exemplary representative of the Church—a kind of living testimony to Catholic beliefs and values. With all my faults, I work pretty hard at it, too. But time and again the authorities have pulled the rug out from under me. The sex abuse scandal isn't the whole of it, but it's made things far worse. Really, I ask you—when you've got something like *that* hanging over your head, how can you put a good face on being Catholic in the eyes of people who are at best suspicious of the Church? (personal communication)

It is questionable whether most Church leaders grasp the depth of the disillusionment among people like this. They have not quit the Church, and they are not likely to. But the anger and alienation regarding the leadership is just below the surface. At the top of the hierarchical structure, one hears self-congratulating talk about the progress that has been made and the newfound commitment to transparency. But many practicing Catholics are furious and mistrustful, even though they are too polite to tell the people at the top what they really think (or else the system simply does not give them the opportunity of doing that).

As for those who have more or less given up on religious practice, it is undoubtedly often true that clergy sex abuse and episcopal cover-up merely supply material for rationalizing something some were on the way to doing anyway—namely, quitting the Church. But that cannot be taken for granted in all cases. Moreover, even when these people are rationalizing, the anger and alienation are still very real. Sex abuse and cover-up did not cause all this by themselves, but they brought a lot of it to the surface and forged it into a powerful destructive force.

Some two years after the scandal erupted, I published an "open letter" to the bishops that made a plea for openness, honesty, and accountability in Church affairs.[2] I was bowled over by the outpouring of responses I received (but not a single one from any bishop and only one from a priest) and by the intensity of the feelings they revealed.

"We're all sinners and we all make mistakes and I can forgive that", one said. "What's tough to take from anyone is when they won't admit that they are making a mistake." Another, citing the anonymous layman mentioned above whom I had quoted in what I wrote, said: "I could relate so well to that lay person's feelings.... I expect secular society to undermine the Church, but when it comes from within it's especially demoralizing."

One of the most substantive responses came from a layman who had worked for a Church-related organization for many years.

> I agree that the bishops are facing a very large problem and that it has existed for a long time. The clerical culture can probably only exist behind a veil that encourages a superstitious reverence. If it were open, only truly spiritual pastors would have a claim on our fealty, and few would qualify. The cloak of secrecy, in my view, is a survival tool. What the scandal did was shine a light on the reality of clerical culture. (personal communication)

In some ways, that comment is too strong for my taste. But whether it is too strong or just right, it is deeply disturbing that a serious lay Catholic who works for the Church could say it.

Dealing with attitudes like these and with the conditions in the Church that they reflect requires a lot more than the policies and structures for child protection that have been

[2] See Russell Shaw, "An Open Letter to America's Bishops", *Crisis*, June 2004.

put in place in dioceses and schools in the last several years. Serious as it is, child abuse nonetheless is just part of the problem discussed here, and protecting children is just another part of what must be done. There is an urgent need for across-the-board openness and accountability at all levels and in all institutions of the Catholic Church. Openness and accountability are by no means the whole remedy for what ails American Catholicism (at its root, the disease concerns faith and its living out), but no other answer will do much good without them.

What We Need to Do Now

Among the steps that should be taken are these:

- Make openness to journalists and observers the rule at general meetings of the United States Conference of Catholic Bishops, with executive sessions limited to matters that truly must be discussed behind closed doors for the good of the Church.
- Adopt and observe a policy of openness in conducting the business of all dioceses and parishes and religious institutes. This includes such sensitive matters as publishing detailed, comprehensive financial reports and letting people in on the studies and planning that precede decisions about parish closings.
- Make a fresh start with diocesan and parish pastoral councils and finance councils, giving these bodies a real say in policy making and making their membership and their agendas and minutes a matter of public record.
- Implement new procedures that, without infringing on the right of the pope to name bishops and the right of bishops to name pastors, give qualified lay

people (and priests and religious) a consultative voice in these processes.

- Liberate the diocesan press so that Catholic newspapers are no longer just house organs but serve as honest sources of reliable factual information and responsible commentary and as vehicles for public opinion.
- Practice consistent, exceptionless honesty in the media relations of the Church at all levels.
- Adopt and implement meaningful freedom-of-information policies in parishes, dioceses, and national Church organizations. The policy statements should be in writing and publicly available.
- Make innovative and sophisticated use of the potential of the Internet as a channel for two-way interactivity in communication, consultation, and governance, from the level of the local parish to the level of the Holy See.
- Undertake ongoing theological research concerning the implications of Vatican Council II's ecclesiology of communion for internal and external communication by the Church.
- Face up to the destructive impact that clericalism continues to have on Catholic life and take the steps necessary to root out clericalist attitudes, structures, and practices once and for all.

Reviving Shared Responsibility

There also is a need to revive the idea of shared responsibility and to renovate existing structures and create new ones for practicing it. This is a large and complicated subject that requires separate examination.

Shared responsibility refers to the participation of lay people and other nonbishops in decision making in the Church. In modern times it was linked to the Second Vatican Council and its teaching about the Church and the role of the laity. But the practice of shared responsibility has historical antecedents that go far back. For many centuries, as we have seen, lay involvement in the choice of bishops, at least by way of consent, was taken for granted; for centuries, too, lay people attended Church councils, frequently taking part in a consultative role. The First Vatican Council was departing from precedent in having no laity present—"in any capacity whatever", Yves Congar says.

Congar writes that lay people are at Church councils "in order that what should be everybody's concern should in fact become so; they are there in order that the community may be able to express its views in whatever affects them, may know what is being dealt with, may act in accordance with the council's decisions and give them full effect." [3] Vatican II returned to the earlier practice, at least in part, by inviting lay persons to be present in the limited role of auditors.

Vatican Council II makes the crucial point that the secular world is the primary and special setting for lay participation in the mission of the Church; the laity have the "special vocation" of making the Church "present and fruitful in those places and circumstances where it is only through them that she can become the salt of the earth". [4] But even so, "the laity too have parts of their own to play" in ecclesial affairs, and for this reason bishops and priests are to "work as brothers with the laity in the Church and for the

[3] Yves Congar, O.P., *Lay People in the Church*, revised edition (London: Geoffrey Chapman, 1985), 251.

[4] Vatican Council II, Dogmatic Constitution on the Church, *Lumen Gentium* (November 21, 1964), no. 33.

Church".[5] The Council speaks specifically in this context
of diocesan and parish councils.[6] Shared responsibility
expresses this spirit.

But if sharing responsibility with the laity goes back a
long way, so does clericalism's resistance to the idea. This
history includes the long struggle during the Middle Ages
focused on the abuse called "lay investiture" that saw lay
lords naming bishops and pastors. Lay trusteeism in the
Church in the United States in the eighteenth and nineteenth centuries was a similar aberration. It is worth considering the lessons of trusteeism here.

Through much of the nineteenth century, councils of the
American bishops denounced trusteeism and called for measures to stamp it out.[7] Most bishops were glad to comply.
The notable exception was in the Diocese of Charleston,
South Carolina, where Bishop John England adopted a diocesan constitution providing for a collaborative system of diocesan and parish governance in which lay people played an
active role. The Vatican said it had no problem with the
Charleston arrangements, but no other American diocese
attempted anything similar. The experiment ended with
Bishop England's death in 1842.[8]

[5] Vatican Council II, Decree on the Apostolate of the Laity, *Apostolicam
Actuositatem* (November 18, 1965), no. 25.

[6] Ibid., no. 26.

[7] Ironically, shifting ownership of Church property to the diocesan bishop
as "corporation sole" set the stage for the argument heard today that parishes
should be included in diocesan settlements with victims of clergy sex abuse
on the theory that the bishop owns the parish property. This is a case of the
solution to one problem leading to another. Many dioceses or parishes lately
have undone, or are now in the process of undoing, what was done in an
earlier century to combat lay trusteeism.

[8] The story is told in many histories of American Catholicism. See, for
example, Peter Clarke, "John England: Missionary to America, Then and

Steps toward creating a system recalling the Charleston experiment were taken at the national level immediately after Vatican II. Central to the new thinking was the creation in 1966 of the National Conference of Catholic Bishops (NCCB), the canonical episcopal conference for the United States mandated by the Council, together with a sister organization, the United States Catholic Conference (USCC). The NCCB was an instrument for cooperative activity by the bishops in areas of their pastoral responsibility (doctrine, liturgy, canon law, seminaries, etc.); only bishops could be members of its policy-formulating committees. The USCC reflected the Church's engagement with a range of issues in secular society (social justice, education, communications); priests, deacons, religious, and lay people served alongside bishops as full, voting members of its committees.

Significant, too, was the creation of a national advisory council, with similarly "mixed" membership. This body was empowered to make recommendations to the USCC—and eventually to the NCCB—concerning policy and programs. One long-range aim was to facilitate the emergence of a national pastoral council—bishops, priests, deacons, religious, and laity working together and exemplifying the principle of shared responsibility in operation.[9]

The process was brought to a sharp halt in the early 1970s by a Vatican letter to the world's bishops strongly discouraging steps in the direction of national pastoral councils in

Now", in *Patterns of Episcopal Leadership*, ed. Gerald P. Fogarty, S.J. (New York: Macmillan Publishing, 1989), 68–84.

[9] These developments are described in papers collected in Michael J. Sheehan and Russell Shaw, eds., *Shared Responsibility at Work: The Catholic Bishops' Advisory Council, 1969–1974* (Washington: United States Catholic Conference, 1975).

response to abuses in several places. Ironically, in the United States the concept received an apparently fatal blow in 1976 from a national assembly under the bishops' sponsorship that culminated in the hierarchy's contribution to the American bicentennial.

This was the famous Call to Action conference, apparently intended as a prototype national pastoral council (though without the name). It was held in Detroit on October 21–23, 1976, after a lengthy, well-publicized buildup that included a series of "hearings" in several parts of the country whose ostensible purpose was to assemble elements of a social action plan for the Church.

As it turned out, a majority of the thirteen hundred delegates in Detroit were employees of dioceses or Church agencies. The conservative writer Russell Kirk, there as a journalist, mischievously called them "church mice".[10] On this occasion, though, the mice decided to roar, and in resolutions whose topics ranged from birth control to the arms race, they called for women's ordination, married priests, the admission of divorced and remarried Catholics to the sacraments, a national arbitration board empowered to undo bishops' decisions, and much else.[11]

As this account suggests, the Call to Action conference was thoroughly botched. "If this is what shared responsibility is like," many people undoubtedly thought, "I want no part of it." And they were right—that is, *if* Call to Action was a fair sample of shared responsibility at work.

[10] Russell Kirk, *The Sword of Imagination: Memoirs of a Half-Century of Literary Conflict* (Grand Rapids, Mich.: William B. Eerdmans Publishing, 1995), 427.

[11] See Russell Shaw, "Time to Dust Off the National Pastoral Council?" *America*, May 28, 2001.

Cooperation in Governance

But the principle of shared responsibility still deserves consideration without being tarred with the very real blunders of the past, and the structures and processes for lay participation that already exist—parish and diocesan councils and the United States Conference of Catholic Bishops' advisory council—need to be strengthened and renewed. Here are some reflections bearing on that.

In the Catholic Church the power of governance is linked to Holy Orders. Canon 129.1 says: "In accord with the prescriptions of law, those who have received sacred orders are capable of the power of governance, which exists in the Church by divine institution and is also called the power of jurisdiction." But is this an exclusive linkage? May *only* ordained persons participate in governance? Evidently not, for canon 129.2 adds: "Lay members of the Christian faithful can cooperate in the exercise of this power in accord with the norm of law."

The hierarchical structure of the Church, divinely given as that structure is, places necessary limits on the role of the laity in governance. Nevertheless, their cooperation is possible. Cooperation in governance can be of three kinds: cooperation as staff; cooperation by consultation; and what one writer lumps together generically as "other forms"— namely, "electoral participation" and "informative participation" (the sharing of views contemplated by those who speak about public opinion, and also expert testimony).[12] Cooperation by consultation is the preeminent way for the laity to be involved in Church governance.

---

[12] Juan Ignacio Arrieta, *Governance Structures within the Catholic Church* (Montreal: Wilson and Lafleur, 2000), 38–41.

Bishops and other pastors obviously have to make decisions; but in doing so, they need to learn about the morally acceptable options and the pros and cons of each, including especially various facts about the capacities of those who would carry them out and those who would be served. Acquiring this information absolutely requires consulting the faithful, as well as—sometimes—experts. Having obtained all this information, the decision makers then should attempt to discern what it is *Christ* wants. At the end, they (or he) needs to be able to say, "Having done the best I could to get information, and then having prayed, I now am convinced that *this* is the option to which the Lord is calling us together."

A sympathetic bishop with whom I was sharing some thoughts about clericalism and lay participation once remarked, "If what you say were carried out with the help of lay Catholics like yourself, it would be good. But I'm afraid it would be done by people ignorant of their own Catholic identity or actively antagonistic to the traditions of the faith."

He had a point. Another bishop with whom I was trading ideas noted the emergence after the abuse scandal of lay protest groups with power-sharing agendas and cited this as an argument against more sharing of responsibility. While agreeing—up to a point—I also noted what I take to be the solution to this particular dilemma. Canon 512.3, on membership in diocesan pastoral councils, says, "No one except Christians of proven faith, good morals and outstanding prudence are to be appointed." If that simple rule were followed, instead of the rule of mindless ideological inclusivism that often appears to underlie the choice of people to advise and collaborate with the hierarchy, all would be well; if it were not, there would be trouble.

Structures and procedures of shared responsibility of any sort should meet the prescription for lay consultation enunciated by Yves Congar:

> [T]hey must not be approached merely as a matter of form, or in some other way that nobody would use if he wants to be understood and followed: the approach must be real. They must be told what is proposed, given so far as possible the reasons for a decision taken, informed about results, difficulties and new measures required; thus may their agreement be obtained and their help enlisted.... This way of going to work always gets results, and no other way does.[13]

At the start of a rightly conducted consultative process, the bishop or other pastor describes the state of affairs he thinks calls for a decision—he shares his thinking about problems and possibilities. He explains that he needs the laity's input about other possibilities and about pros and cons. He makes it clear the decision will not be reached by majority vote, although he wants to know how many people will be affected by one course of action or another. He says he will discern and decide, with the decisive factor being his best understanding of what Jesus wants. Then he will look to the people to accept and cooperate. Everything will take place openly and on the record.

. . .

There are no panaceas. Honest communication is a necessary part of real-world Church communion, but it is not a foolproof guarantee of success. "Everyone should bear in

[13] Congar, *Lay People in the Church*, 269.

mind communication's imperfections", Germain Grisez says. Natural limitations, mistakes, moral faults, and the deficiencies of language and other media ensure that much communication will fail entirely and even partially successful communication will often end in such misunderstanding that "those who communicate regret having done so." [14] Ending the abuse of secrecy in the Church will not change that, since it is part of the fallen human condition.

But let us not end on a negative note. Instead, let us recall the vision of an open Church in *Novo Millennio Ineunte* (At the Beginning of the New Millennium).

In this great-hearted apostolic letter for the Jubilee Year 2000, Pope John Paul II speaks about the "spirituality of communion".[15] In its absence, he says, "external structures of communion ... would become mechanisms without a soul, 'masks' of communion rather than its means of expression and growth." Yet, assuming its indispensable presence, the structures are of great importance. Indeed, "the new century will have to see us more than ever intent on valuing and developing the forms and structures which, in accordance with the Second Vatican Council's major directives, serve to ensure and safeguard communion."

First among these on John Paul's list are the Petrine ministry of the pope and episcopal collegiality, then come the Roman Curia, the Synod of Bishops, and the national conferences of bishops. There is "certainly much more to be done, in order to realize all the potential of these instruments of communion", the Holy Father remarks. Then he says:

[14] Germain Grisez, *The Way of the Lord Jesus*, vol. 2, *Living a Christian Life* (Quincy, Ill.: Franciscan Press, 1993), 393.
[15] See Pope John Paul II, apostolic letter *Novo Millennio Ineunte* (At the Beginning of the New Millennium) (January 6, 2001), nos. 43–45.

Communion must be cultivated and extended day by day and at every level in the structures of each church's life. There, relations between bishops, priests and deacons, between pastors and the entire People of God, between clergy and religious, between associations and ecclesial movements must all be clearly characterized by communion. To this end, the structures of participation envisaged by canon law, such as the council of priests and the pastoral council, must be ever more highly valued. These of course are not governed by the rules of parliamentary democracy, because they are consultative rather than decision-making;[16] yet this does not mean that they are less meaningful and relevant. The theology and spirituality of communion encourage a fruitful dialogue between pastors and faithful: on the one hand uniting them a priori in all that is essential, and on the other leading them to pondered agreement in matters open to discussion.

We need to make our own the ancient pastoral wisdom which, without prejudice to their authority, encouraged pastors to listen more widely to the entire People of God. Significant is Saint Benedict's reminder to the abbot of a monastery, inviting him to consult even the youngest members of the community: "By the Lord's inspiration, it is often a younger person who knows what is best." And Saint Paulinus

---

[16] The Latin is: "*consulendi ... non autem decernendi*". The English translation released by the Vatican renders this as "consultative rather than deliberative", but the correct translation, as here, is "consultative rather than decision-making". Germain Grisez (personal correspondence) suggests that the error can be traced to the Latin text of the 1997 Vatican document "On Certain Questions regarding the Collaboration of the Non-Ordained Faithful in the Sacred Ministry of the Priest", to which the papal document makes a footnote reference here. The point is important. Consultation that does not contribute to deliberation is meaningless. In order to deliberate well, people in authority must engage in consultation, of which information gathering is part. Excluding lay people from participating in the deliberation that is part of pastoral governance means excluding them from having any meaningful input. But this is not what the pope says. Rather, he is distinguishing, correctly, between being consulted and making decisions.

of Nola urges: "Let us listen to what all the faithful say, because in every one of them the Spirit of God breathes."

While the wisdom of the law, by providing precise rules for participation, attests to the hierarchical structure of the Church and averts any temptation to arbitrariness or unjustified claims, the spirituality of communion, by prompting a trust and openness wholly in accord with the dignity and responsibility of every member of the People of God, supplies institutional reality with a soul. (no. 45)

Communication is difficult, even in the Church, but the consequences of not communicating, to say nothing of lies, equivocation, self-serving and manipulative secrecy, nonaccountability—the sad litany of communication faults—are worse: loss of trust, anger, alienation, unraveling of lived communion. Failures of communication must be overcome, not multiplied by concealment and dissimulation.

In this way we express the reality of the Church, which at one and the same time is the spotless bride of Christ and a band of sinners. The Church's failings are our failings. When we speak of reforming the Church by honest, open communication and accountability, we are speaking of reforming ourselves. And always we have before us the consolation of knowing that, as Saint Josemaria Escriva says:

All this is true, but it does not authorize us in any way to judge the Church in a human manner, without theological faith. We cannot consider only the greater or lesser merits of certain churchmen or other Christians. To do this would be to limit ourselves to the surface of things. *What is most important in the Church is not how we humans react, but how God acts.*[17]

[17] Saint Josemaria Escriva, "The Great Unknown", in *Christ Is Passing By* (Mandaluyong, Metro Manila: Sinag-Tala Publishers, 1977), 178 (italics added).

INDEX

confidentiality, rights to, 22–24,
    125–27
Congar, Yves, 140n36, 147, 155,
    161
consent, manufacture of, 109
consequentialist approach of Bok,
    125–26
conservative Catholicism,
    concerns of, 37
control and manipulation, secrecy
    as instrument of, 31
1 Corinthians
    11:17–20, 145–46
    12:11, 142
    14:2–4, 146
    14:23–25, 146
La Croix, 57–58
culture of secrecy in Church.
    See secrecy in Catholic
    Church

The Da Vinci Code (Brown),
    7–8
Dalgairns, J.D., 41
Davidson, James D., 33–34
democracy
    accountability in, 134–36
    Church distinguished from, 9,
        133–36
    freedom of the press,
        42–44, 51–52, 120–22,
        128–31
    openness and transparency
        assumed by, 34
    privacy, importance of, 22–23
diocesan councils, shared
    responsibility in, 113–17, 138,
    154–61
diocesan press, 103–5

disciplina arcani, 24
doctrine of social communication
    Communio et Progressio, 28n13,
        61, 76–78, 83, 99–100, 133,
        147n47
    in interconciliar years, 51–53
    at Vatican II, 60–64
Döllinger, Johannes, 49, 51
Dominici Gregis, 27n12
Dulles, Avery, 141

Ecclesiam Suam, 63–64
ecclesiology
    communio, Church as, 9,
        117–18, 119, 143–47
    sex abuse scandal and Church
        structure, 90–91
Elders, Leo, 129n18
England, John, 156
Ephesus, Council of, 41
episcopate. *See* bishops
Escriva, Josemaria, 164
Eternal Word Television Network
    (EWTN), 79
Ethics in Communications,
    100–101, 131–33
Eucharist in early Church,
    concealment from
    nonbaptized of, 24
EWTN (Eternal Word Television
    Network), 79
Ex Corde Ecclesiae, 65–66
external communications. *See*
    media relations

Felici, Pericle, 56
finances of Church
    accountability for, 139

finances of Church (*continued*)
  Boston Archdiocese, financial
    report released by,
    29–30n16, 97–98
  diocesan and parish councils,
    shared responsibility in,
    113–17, 138, 154–61
  sex abuse scandal, effects of,
    150
First Vatican Council, 46–51, 155
Franz Joseph (Holy Roman
    Emperor), 28n12
freedom of the press, 42–44,
    51–52, 120–22, 128–31

Galatians 3:28, 142
Gallagher, Raymond, 74
Gaudium et Spes, 62
Gauthé, Gilbert, 87
general meetings of U.S. bishops,
    65–85
  advantages of open meetings
    for bishops, 79
  anonymity of balloting at,
    69–70
  criteria for secrecy, failure to
    disclose or explain, 127
  Dallas 2002 meeting, 78–79,
    86–87
  decision to open meeting to
    press (1969–1972), 71–76
  Ex Corde Ecclesia vote, 65–69
  issues of openness and secrecy
    at, 67–71
  Latin, remarks at first open
    meeting in (1972), 75
  private executive sessions,
    growing length of
    (1990's-2007), 80–82

  process of holding open
    meeting, 78–79
  reasons for opening of, 76–78
  reasons for reclosing of, 82–85,
    132
  sex abuse scandal addressed at,
    78, 81, 86–87
Golden Rule, 124
governance, Church powers of,
    159–61
Gregory XVI (pope), 42–43, 128
Gregory, Wilton, 86
Grisez, Germain, 120–25, 162
group secrecy vs. individual
    privacy, 125–27

happy talk and spin, 108–13
Häring, Bernard, 31, 113
Hecker, Isaac, 47n14
Henn, William, 118, 142–43
hierarchical structure of Church
  accountability and, 140–43
  governance, cooperation in,
    159
higher education, Catholic, and
  Ex Corde Ecclesiae, 65–66
history of secrecy in Catholic
  Church, 39–64
  doctrine of social communica-
    tion, development of,
    51–53
  freedom of the press and
    Anti-Catholicism in 19th
    century, 42–44
  lay trusteeism, 45–46
  Newman on consulting the
    laity, 39–42
  Vatican I, 46–51
  Vatican II. *See* Vatican II